A Two-Year-Old goes to Nursery School

Elisheva Gertner

A Two-Year-Old
goes to
Nursery School

A Case Study of Separation Reactions

MARJORIE GRAHAM JANIS

TAVISTOCK PUBLICATIONS

First published in 1964
by Tavistock Publications (1959) Limited
11 New Fetter Lane, London E.C.4

Printed in Great Britain
in 12 on 13 point Bembo
by Billing & Sons Limited
Guildford and London
and bound by
W. & J. Mackay & Company Limited
Rochester, Kent

To Lottie
and her family

Contents

Acknowledgements

This study was undertaken as part of my work in the Masters Program of Bank Street College of Education, New York City.

I wish to thank Dr Barbara Biber of Bank Street College of Education, and my husband, Dr Irving L. Janis of Yale University, for their valuable suggestions and criticisms.

Special thanks are due to Lottie's nursery-school teacher, who must remain anonymous, for her insightful contributions. I am extremely indebted to Miss Eveline Omwake of Yale University Child Study Center for her generous help on many phases of the study.

The investigation could not have been made without the full and enthusiastic cooperation that Lottie's mother gave to it. I also wish to express my gratitude to both Lottie's parents for opening their home to me as an 'inside observer', and for their critical review of the first draft of the manuscript.

Personae

Lottie's Family
LOTTIE—two years and three months at the start of the study
in September 1956
DORRIE, her sister—five years and eight months
HEIDI, her sister—ten years and four months
MRS BAKER, her mother
MR BAKER, her father

Lottie's Nursery School
MISS WILKINS, Lottie's teacher
MRS ZERBER, the assistant teacher

My Family
CARON, my five-year-old daughter
KAYE, my thirteen-year-old daughter
IRVING, my husband
MARJORIE, the investigator

I

Prologue

In September 1956 Lottie's mother decided to send her to nursery school. She had not originally planned to do so. Lottie was only two years and three months of age and her mother felt that it would be better to wait until the middle of the school year. However, the school had so many applicants that a child had to be enrolled in the two-year-old group at the beginning of the year in order to obtain a place. This was one factor in Mrs Baker's decision.

Mrs Baker also took account of Lottie's strong disconsolate reaction to the absence of her two older sisters at school. Dorrie, who was five and a half years old, had just started public school kindergarten and was away all morning. Heidi, ten years old, had a full day in the fifth grade at the same neighborhood school. And Lottie, left behind, wandered through the empty rooms calling, "Where are the 'chilldies'? Where are the 'chilldies'?" She could not settle down to play, either with the abundant supply of toys in the room she shared with Dorrie, or outside in the well-equipped, but now deserted, back-yard.

Through the summer months this yard had been a buzzing, bustling place. Children from two to thirteen years of age gathered here, morning, afternoon, and evening. There was a preponderance of girls. But boys dashed in, too, for a quick game of tag or ball, and whipped off again. Lottie had been in the midst of it,

I

the youngest (the next in age was four). She watched; she joined in; she was free to come and go—into the house, too, if necessary. She was usually both accepted and protected by the changing group, and especially by her two older sisters.

Now they were all in school. And there were no neighboring young children to play with.

THE NURSERY SCHOOL

Mrs Baker was fortunate in having available a fine nursery school in a nearby city, fifteen minutes' drive from the house. Lottie's sister Dorrie had attended this school for three years: first in the two-year-old group, meeting just twice a week for two and a half hours; then in the 'threes', for three mornings a week; the last year Dorrie had gone five mornings in the four-year-old group. Lottie had often accompanied her mother to drop Dorrie off and to call for her. She had explored and handled almost everything in Dorrie's room. She was especially at home in the playground with the stairs and swings, boxes and boards, jungle gym, and sandpile. In the spring there had been rabbits living outside in a cage. In the playground, during the often leisurely pick-up time, she had inveigled innumerable "one more turns".[1] She knew well Miss Peters, Dorrie's teacher, and many of the children in the group. Going out of the building, she never failed to dash wildly down the hall with the others to the last heavy door, to hoist herself up by the metal bar, hanging on tightly for the swinging ride that came when an adult pushed.

This year, Lottie would go to the room next door to Dorrie's old room. The playground for the 'twos' was adjacent to that for the 'fours', set off by a fence. Miss Wilkins (who had taught Dorrie when she was two and three years old) would be Lottie's teacher.

[1] For the purpose of clarity, double quotation marks are used to indicate words and phrases actually spoken by the people appearing in the study; single quotation marks are used to distinguish technical terms, colloquialisms, and any expressions that have a special meaning.

It was the school's policy to make a gradual transition for the child beginning in school. The mother was invited to come and stay with the child until he seemed at home there and ready to stay by himself.

II

Purpose and Plan

When Mrs Baker told me that she was going to send Lottie to school, I discussed with her the possibility of keeping a record of Lottie's experience of beginning school, with special emphasis on her reactions and behavior at home during the adjustment period. It seemed to be a rare opportunity to gain insight into some of the specific ways in which a child handles the first two major, linked steps towards independence from the family: first, the initial recurrent, routinized separation from the mother; and second, regular attendance at a place away from home, peopled by a large peer group, in the care of unfamiliar adults.

My interest in the psychological problems of mother-child separation was stimulated by the work of Dr John Bowlby and his associates at the Tavistock Clinic in London. Particularly, James Robertson's studies of hospitalization as a separation experience led me to the question of how young children cope with less dramatic separations such as those that occur when they first begin school.

OBSERVATIONAL STANDPOINT

Relationship with Lottie's Family

In the growing number of studies in recent years on mother-child separation, there has been a dearth of detailed material on reactions of normal children in the home to the first usual, everyday

4

separation experiences. It is obviously very difficult to place an observer in the home for this purpose. If it were possible, it would be hard to do so for sufficiently frequent and extended periods. Moreover, one would expect the presence of a strange observer to have some indeterminable effect on the observed.

Because of my close friendship with the Baker family, I saw Lottie almost every day, either at her home or at mine. The Baker family and my family had known each other for ten years. They functioned for the children somewhat like extended families. The three Baker girls and my two daughters often ate and played, and sometimes slept, at each other's houses. The two families went on special excursions together and shared many family and holiday celebrations. Kaye, my older daughter of thirteen, was a special friend of ten-year-old Heidi Baker. Caron, my five-year-old, was the best friend of Dorrie Baker who was five and a half. Dorrie and Caron had been classmates at nursery school for three years, but now were attending different public school kindergartens. And Lottie—from infancy—had been handled, watched, played with, teased, and cared for by my family as well as her own.

The 'Inside Observer'

This close relationship facilitated almost daily observation. It was taken for granted that I might be present at any time—during meals, play, bathroom and bedtime routines, shopping, and excursions. It also meant, however, that I was often a 'participant observer'; and further, all the material gathered must be understood as having been screened through the eyes of an inside observer with a deep personal attachment to Lottie and her family.

Inside observation makes available for research the intimate, detailed home life and behavior of the normal child. Currently, children are studied in a wide variety of ways: school observations, tests of many kinds, projective techniques, and experimental procedures are all employed. But, by and large, investi-

B

gation of the child's behavior within his family is limited to the occasional parental interview or home visit.

When inside observation is used, techniques must be developed to take into account requirements of objectivity which are more readily fulfilled in studies that do not involve a personal relationship between investigator and subject. In this study the collection of the data was completely separated in time from the analysis of the material. The observations and reports were filed away as they came. Not only was no effort made to seek out interpretations during the year of the study, but, surprisingly enough, there was little or no awareness at the time of what subsequently emerged from the detailed review of the material. A year of residence abroad intervened, when I did not see Lottie or her family, before work on the study was resumed. Thus, the final analysis was based entirely on the written records; there was no intrusion of unrecorded impressions or of contact with Lottie a as three-year-old.

No attempt was made in this work to describe the personalities of the parents or to interpret their behavior with the child. Nevertheless, it seems to me that the quality of the mother-child relationship is conveyed by the material. The investigation was focused by design on the child's reactions and behavior. In these particular circumstances there were only a few restrictions imposed by my friendship with the family and the need to protect their privacy. (For example, the ways in which Lottie may have been affected by her father's work could not be discussed.)

THE STUDY MATERIAL

Role of the Mother

In recent years there has been a great awareness of the distortions of emotion and memory that a mother's reports on her child may contain. But this unique source can provide important information, and, it seeems to me, has not been sufficiently employed in the study of young children. If the mother is used primarily as an informant of on-going behavior, and if her reports are supple-

6

mented by direct home observations, then many of the short-comings can be minimized.

Lottie's mother agreed readily to the study and she was willing to take an essential part in gathering the material. She reported on every nursery-school session, including what occurred before and after school. Further, Mrs Baker described home incidents and changing routines as they happened over the months of the study, so that it was possible to build up a detailed picture of Lottie at home, during her first year at nursery school.

The mother's role in the study was structured as one of informant. Her reports were obtained under special interview conditions to facilitate recall and to keep the study procedures as separate as possible from other aspects of my close relationship to the Baker family.

On the days that Lottie attended nursery school, I interviewed Mrs Baker in the early afternoon while Lottie was having her nap. First, Mrs Baker reported, while I recorded, what had happened before, during, and after school. Then followed an 'inquiry', in which I asked for clarification or further information, where available. It was also at this time, mainly, that Mrs Baker recounted home events and described daily routines.

The majority of these interviews were conducted within a few hours of the school session, while the events described were clearly in mind. Sometimes this was not possible, and a day or two elapsed between the session and the report, rarely more.

I questioned Mrs Baker, after the study was completed, concerning her reactions to having taken part in the investigation. She expressed positive feelings about her participation. She termed its function for her as a "catharsis", not a "treatment"; she felt it had not determined any course of action. Although she now wished that she had used it as an aid in her handling of Lottie's difficulties, she asserted: "I didn't use it that way at all."

Nursery-school Observations

The nursery-school material was, of necessity, limited in scope. Mrs Baker had no formal training in nursery education, but she

7

had acquired considerable previous experience as a mother in nursery school with her two older daughters. She had also assisted for a time in a cooperative nursery school. However, she was put into a very active participating role by Lottie at the start of the school period; and, as Lottie became more familiar with school, Mrs Baker deliberately withdrew to the sidelines as much as possible, often out of sight or hearing range of Lottie. Furthermore, she gradually increased her time away from school; occasionally one of the teachers would give her a brief summary of Lottie's morning, on her return. Thus, as the year progressed, the school material became increasingly restricted to details of arrival and departure.

In June 1957, at the close of the school year, I was fortunate in obtaining an interview with Miss Wilkins, Lottie's skilled and experienced teacher. This material filled in gaps in the school observations and provided valuable insights and hypotheses about Lottie's adjustment to nursery school.

At the beginning of the year (September 1956), Miss Wilkins agreed to let me come into school with Mrs Baker and Lottie, as an observer. This was tried for only part of the first morning. It became immediately apparent that it would not be possible for me to remain in the background in school because Lottie drew me persistently into her activities. Miss Wilkins, Mrs Baker, and I all felt that it would be distracting and confusing for Lottie to have me there. And so the plan for direct school observations was dropped. Occasionally I went with Mrs Baker to call for Lottie and could observe how Lottie greeted her mother and left school. Also, I obtained visual (no sound) observations of three early sessions through the door-window of school.

The Study Records

The study was originally planned to cover the initial adjustment period, which was expected to last from one to three months, with a follow-up toward the end of the school year. Lottie's own concerted efforts to work her way out of a complicated and

8

difficult dilemma induced me to extend the study. It stretched throughout the school year.

The main material was gathered from 17 September 1956 to 10 June 1957. Lottie was two years and three months at the beginning, three years old at the end. She attended, in all, fifty-one sessions of nursery school. The two-year-olds (a group of twelve children) met Tuesdays and Thursdays for two and a half hours each morning. There were two long school vacations—three weeks at Christmas time and more than two weeks in the early spring. Lottie was absent from school for three sessions because of colds and she missed six sessions because of transportation difficulties (including the week she was away on a family trip).

In summary, the study material comprises: (1) my direct home observations (from two to five each week); (2) reports by Lottie's mother on the nursery-school sessions and home behavior; and (3) an interview at the end of the school year with Lottie's nursery-school teacher.

ORGANIZATION OF THE BOOK

Lottie will be introduced as she appeared at the time that school began—lunching at home with her family, visiting school, and attending the opening session. Then some of the background will be filled in with descriptions of Lottie, her place in the family group, her home, and some earlier developmental history.

The school year is divided into three parts. In Chapter V, Autumn, the material is presented, in a repeated chronological sequence, under various descriptive headings. The records for this period were the most extensive. Subject-matter categories permit a detailed account of the child's behavior, but they also entail considerable repetition since the divisions overlap to some degree. The themes, expressing principal behavioral convergences, appear and reappear, variously highlighted in each of the successive sections.

A different procedure is followed in Chapters VI and VII, Winter and Spring. Here the records were less abundant. This made it feasible to trace the emerging themes concurrently, in a single chronological sequence.

Throughout the study a number of hypotheses consistent with Freudian theory are introduced. These hypotheses were not originally contemplated but grew directly out of the analysis of the records. It was not the intention of this study, for example, to examine the relevance of psychosexual development to the separation problem. However, I was led into this topic when it became apparent that certain themes could be more clearly understood in the light of Freudian developmental assumptions.

Nevertheless, no attempt was made to examine the material systematically, with respect to all potentially relevant Freudian postulates or to those of other psychological schools, which might have led to additional hypotheses. Although I did not try to impose any particular theory on the case material, my background in psychoanalytic theory undoubtedly sensitized me to certain behavior patterns to which other observers might have attached less importance.

The main hypotheses are summarized and elaborated in Chapter VIII, Discussion and Conclusions. The Epilogue presents follow-up material on Lottie from three to eight years of age, and points out persisting trends.

III

School Begins

We shall see Lottie first as she appeared in the records at the time that school begins. She has lunch at home with her family; she goes to a friend's house with her mother; she is taken to visit nursery school; and she attends the opening session of school.

LOTTIE AT HOME

17 September 1956. Record of Lottie's lunch at home three days before school begins

Lottie is in the dinette off the kitchen of her home. Her sister Dorrie has helped her to wash her hands in the downstairs bathroom. Lottie climbs into her high-chair (without the tray) drawn up at table. Her mother is cooking bacon at the stove. Dorrie and Caron (Dorrie's friend) sit at the table, too, waiting for lunch. (My attention, as recorder, was fixed on Lottie. No attempt was made to catch all the conversation going on around me; sometimes the gist is given, sometimes a quote when Lottie picks it up.)

11:55 a.m.

LOTTIE	I needa bib.
MOTHER	What?
LOTTIE	I wanta bib.
DORRIE	She says she wants a bib.
CARON	Lottie didn't use to want to wear a bib.

11

LOTTIE	Bring me a bib.
MOTHER	You want a bib?
LOTTIE	I wanna bacon. I like bacon! (*Mother gives her a piece.*) I needa bib.
MOTHER	This one? (*Bringing her a bib—putting it on.*)
LOTTIE	That's the right one.

Mother says she is making more bacon, then will make sandwiches.

CARON	Bacon, lettuce, and tomato on white.
DORRIE	Mayonnaise.

(*Lottie eats bacon.*)

MOTHER	Three B L and TS with mayonnaise.
DORRIE	I know how to spell 'kissing': K-I-S-S-I-N-G.
MOTHER	Do you want a straw? What color?
LOTTIE	GREEN! (*Her favorite color.*)
MOTHER	I don't have green; chocolate or strawberry?
LOTTIE	Chocolate. (*Mother brings it and puts it in Lottie's milk glass.*) I want a fresh one. (*The flavor-straw colors and flavors milk as it is sipped.*)
MOTHER	This is fresh.
LOTTIE	Don't bend it. (*Mother hands out strawberry straws to Caron and Dorrie. Lottie watches Caron and Dorrie dipping the straws into their milk.*) Chocolate's coming in too—chocolate's coming in! (*Dips straw up and down in her milk—sips very competently.*) Mmmmmm. More bacon. A big bacon.
MOTHER	All right. (*Hands piece to Lottie.*)

(*Lottie holds the piece of bacon in two hands, bites off piece, then holds it in her right hand.*)

DORRIE	There's blood on my plate. (*Drops of pink milk from her straw.*)

(*Lottie looks over at Dorrie.*)
Mother says no—it is just strawberry color.

MOTHER   Here are napkins. (*Hands out one to each child.*)

(*Lottie fixes her napkin flat on the table next to her plate; she pushes the big plate of tomato and lettuce away to make room for the napkin.*)

LOTTIE   I can't move it over. (*Mother helps; now the napkin is flat next to Lottie's plate.*)

MOTHER   I'll make you a half, O.K.?

DORRIE   Yes.

CARON   Yes.

LOTTIE   Yes.

DORRIE   I'm wiping up blood. (*She wipes up the pink milk on her plate with her napkin.*)

LOTTIE   More bacon.

MOTHER   I'm making you a sandwich.

LOTTIE   I want a sandwich. (*Sips milk.*) Mmmmmm. Mmmmm. (*Her voice starts out high—slides to low.*) Look at the toe nail, Margie. Look at the toe nail. Toe nail. (*Perhaps this refers to the shape of the bacon.*) Give me bacon (*to her mother who is bringing a plate of bacon to the table for making sandwiches*). Ba-a-a-con. Give me bacon (*softly*). (*Mother gives Lottie a piece.*) Give me bacon. (*Lottie grabs a little piece and shoves it into her mouth. She chews, watching me write.*)

Caron says something about her straw.

LOTTIE   That's strawberry, Caron. That's strawberry, Caron! It's strawberry, Caron.

CARON   We know it's strawberry.

12 : 05 p.m.

LOTTIE   More bacon. (*Mother gives her a piece. Lottie watches her mother give Caron and Dorrie their sandwiches.*)

CARON   Oh. Look at my blood (*drops from her strawberry straw*).

13

LOTTIE   I want a big one, Mommy.

MOTHER   Yes.

LOTTIE   I love bacon!

MOTHER   I know.

LOTTIE   Cold!

MOTHER   Is the milk cold?

LOTTIE   Yes. Chocolate might help me (*sips*). (*Mother brings a sandwich to Lottie's plate, cuts it in half.*) Too big— too big. (*Picks up a quarter of the sandwich in her hand.*) I ate the bacon. (*Her first bite out of the sandwich was the bacon.*) Who's doing that? Who's doing that, Margie? Is Mommy doing that?

MOTHER   What?

LOTTIE   That. (*Points to her mother at the other side of the table.*)

MOTHER   I'm making sandwiches.

(*Lottie takes out the lettuce from her sandwich and stuffs it into her mouth. Then she puts a tiny piece of lettuce near the plate in front of me. She takes it right back and eats it.*)

LOTTIE   Mommy, give me those bacons. (*Points to big plate of bacon; she puts down her sandwich.*)

MOTHER   No, Daddy's lunch.

(*Lottie picks up a quarter of the sandwich in her right hand and takes a bite. She listens to Caron and Dorrie talking about playing songs on the piano.*)

LOTTIE   Up again. (*Her father comes in.*) Here, Caron, want this? (*A piece of tomato.*)

CARON   No.

(*Lottie offers it to me; I shake my head.*)

LOTTIE   Here, Mommy. (*She gives the piece of tomato to her mother.*) Margie's having your lunch, your lunch pretty soon. Here we go to nursery school! Here we go to nursery school! Here we go to nursery school! Here we go to nursery school! Here we go to nursery school! Here we go to nursery school! (*She sips her milk.*) I'm popping it up.

MOTHER   Sipping it up.

LOTTIE   I'm popping it up!!

MOTHER   Don't play—drink. That's the way.

(*Caron mentions the word sandwich. Lottie tries to pick up her sandwich.*)

LOTTIE   It's falling, want to take it off. Open it. (*She takes off the top piece of bread and eats the lettuce.*) Ahh. (*She opens her mouth, shows the lettuce inside to Caron and me.*) Hmmm—hmmm (*eating her lettuce, bouncing in her high-chair*).

MOTHER   Don't jump. Finish, darling.

LOTTIE   I'm cold. (*She stops bouncing, picks up a piece of bacon and puts it in her mouth.*) Mmmm—mmmm—mmmm (*bouncing with each sound*). Mmmm.

CARON   Don't, Lottie. She's putting her foot on my lap.

MOTHER   Don't, Lottie.

(*Lottie brings her foot back. She kicks her high-chair lightly, sipping chocolate milk.*)

LOTTIE   Chocolate came in! Chocolate came in, Margie. (*She sips out of the straw. She dips the straw up and down in the glass and blows bubbles through the straw into the milk.*) I can't blow it.

MOTHER   That's blowing it; when you suck it in, it's drinking. (*Caron and Dorrie are blowing bubbles into their milk.*) Don't do it any more—drink it.

LOTTIE   Want bacon right there.

MOTHER   O.K.—one more.

(*Lottie eats the piece of bacon.*)
Dorrie says that she is ready for dessert.

15

LOTTIE Want another bacon. Give me bacon. Give me more. (*Lottie stands up in the high-chair, looks over to the stove.*)

MOTHER This is the last.

LOTTIE Mommy gave me a rocking. Mommy gave me a rocking. (*She holds out a curved piece of bacon.*)

DORRIE Give me one.

MOTHER No more left. (*Lottie reaches to the tomato slices on a big plate.*) You can have a tomato.

LOTTIE Nooo. (*She sips her milk from the straw.*)

DORRIE Dessert.

LOTTIE Dessert. You have chocolate, Caron.

CARON I have strawberry.

LOTTIE You have strawberry. (*She chews on a piece of bacon that she is holding in her hand, laughs at a remark of Dorrie's, then takes hold of Caron's straw.*)

CARON Don't squash. Lottie squashed it! Did you suck it?

LOTTIE No.

DORRIE Dirt—dirt for dessert!

LOTTIE I want dirt too (*smiling*).

CARON I want dirt.

LOTTIE I want dirt.

MOTHER Shall I go outside and get it and put Reddi-Whip on it?

(*Lottie nods, smiling. She spits out the bacon after long chewing.*)

LOTTIE I don't like that. I don't like it.

MOTHER All right—hard piece. Are you through?

LOTTIE No, no (*handing her plate to her mother*). This (*sips milk*).

MOTHER Ready for some dessert?

LOTTIE (*Nods*) I want dirt, dirt, Mommy. I said dirt. Dirt! Dirt! Big dirt.

DORRIE I had a crazy dream. (*Mother brings out ice cream on sticks. She hands them out.*) Thanks a lot, I'm hungry.

LOTTIE I'm hungry. I don't want it down! (*Reaching.*)
I don't eat the paper.

CARON Lottie can push it up herself.

LOTTIE I can push it up.

12 : 20 p.m.

CARON It's cold.

LOTTIE It's too cold for me. Yes, it is too cold.

MOTHER I don't think so.

(*Lottie licks with her tongue— looks at her father and me, laughing.*)

LOTTIE Cold—that's cold. Don't lick a "gol". It's coming out. It's coming out, Mommy.

FATHER She can push it up.

LOTTIE I pushed it up. (*She sticks out her tongue, licks, shows it to her father.*) (*Putting her finger on the red center of ice cream.*) Oh look it—ice cream. I can't suck it. That's a tree (*a picture on the cardboard cylinder around the ice cream; she turns it—looking at it*). Oh, an eye (*a red half-moon on the cardboard*).

MOTHER What is this?

CARON A moon.

LOTTIE An eye.

MOTHER Moon and stars.

LOTTIE Moon and stars.

DORRIE Push it up.

LOTTIE I can push this up. (*She pulls out the stick and pusher.*)

MOTHER Can I put that back?

LOTTIE I took that out!

MOTHER There it is!

LOTTIE Mmmmmm (*eating ice cream*).

CARON Lottie's favorite color.

LOTTIE See my favorite color. (*She squeals, pointing to a picture on the ice cream cardboard.*)

MOTHER   Peter Pan Company (*telling who makes the ice cream*).

LOTTIE   Peter Pan Company. Peter Pan Company. I gotta funny "mace" (for face)—funny face (*laughs*). (*She laughs again.*) I fall down from my high-chair. (*Mother touches Father's shoulder.*) Mommy petting Daddy! (*Lottie opens her mouth with ice cream in it.*) What's this called, Mommy?

MOTHER   Ice cream with jam inside.

LOTTIE   Oh-h, Oh-h, Oh-h. (*Lottie's ice cream comes off the stick.*) I didn't take it off.

MOTHER   No, you didn't.

LOTTIE   Yes I did. (*Mother bumps into birdcage. It swings and the bird flutters.*) Mommy! (*watching her mother at the birdcage*). I put it on a plate.

MOTHER   Do you want it on a plate?

LOTTIE   I take it off. I take it off. I have it that way. (*She puts her arm on the ice cream.*)

MOTHER   Oh—oh.

LOTTIE   I'm cold (*crossing her arms tight across her chest*).

MOTHER   Sweater?

DORRIE   Ice cream would help.

MOTHER   No, it would make her colder.

LOTTIE   I might get coughed and I throw up.

DORRIE   I didn't drip.

LOTTIE   I think these are good! (*eating with a spoon, shaking her head*). I said "joke off her"—really!

12 : 31 p.m.

MOTHER   Get through now. Time to take your nap.

CARON   Lottie's getting long hair (*Mother putting in Lottie's barrette*).

LOTTIE   I need my barrette in. (*Mother and Father discuss Lottie's hair—oiling it, and so forth. Father says that she's had infections in it too.*) Had infections. No more. (*Mother takes her plate away. Lottie stands up in the high-chair. Mother wipes her off and lifts her out.*) Bah. Bah. Bah. Yes. Yes. (*Lottie runs and hugs her father.*) Mommy, pick up. (*Mother does.*) Ahhh.

DORRIE   Cookie.

LOTTIE   Give me a cookie.

MOTHER   Bye, Margie.

LOTTIE   (*Calling out loudly going up the stairs to her nap*) Bye, Margie, I said.

12 : 35 p.m.

Lottie lunching at home, three days before nursery school begins (two years and three months old), is enthusiastic and definite, observing and commenting, verbal (sense and nonsense) and experimental. She has to have some things 'just so'. There is much oral activity—sipping, munching, blowing, tasting, opening and shutting her mouth, spitting out, licking, and a large appetite for what she likes. She makes a laughing, six-times-repeated comment about going to school: "Here we go to nursery school!" Constantly in motion, she touches, handles, bounces, and kicks. She both imitates, especially her sister Dorrie, and initiates. She enjoys and creates humorous situations and remarks, laughs freely and frequently. Her independence striving is strong; she wants to do it herself and triumphs in her own accomplishments. But she also accepts help for some things, and she can be a little girl going to bed—in her mother's arms.

Lottie cannot be ignored. By her lively observation and participation in all that goes on, she almost always takes her place at the center of things. And though she may elicit exasperation at times, the dominant atmosphere in her family group is one of appreciation, care, and delight.

AWAY FROM HOME

18 September 1956. Record of visit, dancing school, talk about nursery school

Mrs Baker reports that she took Lottie with her to visit friends of hers. (Lottie had seen them for short visits, mostly at

19

her house, several times in the last year.) Lottie was extremely shy and quiet, and clung to her mother almost the whole time. (The boy there also stayed close to his mother.) The friend was in a new house. She has two boys: one a few months older than Lottie, Danny (who is much bigger and rougher); the other a baby, in whom Lottie showed much greater interest. Toward the end of the visit Lottie played a little bit with Danny.

Last week Lottie was driving with Dorrie, Caron, Kaye, and me (back from Caron's school) very happily. But when I stopped to pick up an eight-year-old neighborhood boy, who got into the front, Lottie cried and clung to Dorrie. She did not stop for about five minutes, until the boy got out at his house.

In the afternoon (18 September) Lottie went with her mother, myself, Dorrie, and Caron to dancing school where she stayed and watched Dorrie's and Caron's ballet class, as she had done many times during the previous year.

Mrs Baker told Lottie that they would go to nursery school tomorrow for a visit to see Miss Wilkins (her teacher):

LOTTIE   I don't like Miss Wilkins.
MOTHER   Why not? You don't know her. *I* like Miss Wilkins.
LOTTIE   You like Miss Wilkins, Mommy?
MOTHER   Yes.
LOTTIE   Mommy, you going to be there? I don't want no Mommy at nursery school. I need my Mommy.

Mrs Baker assured Lottie this was just a short visit to see her room and to meet Miss Wilkins, and that Mother would stay with her the whole time.

Lottie is shy and clings to her mother when visiting a friend who has a boy of her own age. She cries hard when a strange, older boy gets into the car with her. She talks about visiting nursery school with her mother and says that she does not like her teacher, Miss Wilkins. She states clearly her need to have

her mother stay with her at school: "Mommy, you going to be
there? I don't want no Mommy at nursery school. I need my
Mommy."

VISIT TO SCHOOL

*19 September 1956. Record of Lottie's visit to nursery school the
day before the first session*

While she was getting ready to go to nursery school Lottie
said, "I love Miss Wilkins." Mrs Baker took Lottie to visit
the nursery school so that she could meet Miss Wilkins
and the other teachers and see her room (no other children
were there). They waited outside in the waiting room for
fifteen minutes. Lottie played happily, saying "hello" to
everybody, petting a baby. When they went into the room
with Miss Wilkins, Lottie took her mother's hand. Then she
left her mother in the room to go over to the doll corner;
she made judgements on the dolls there: "I like this one.
Don't like this one." She found a pile of colored plastic
spoons which she liked. She went over to the blocks and the
rubber animals—pointed them out (they were not handled—
only the dolls and spoons were handled). She came back to
the table and sat on her mother's lap. Mrs Baker and Miss
Wilkins were talking all this time with Lottie edging her
way into the conversation. Another teacher slipped in;
Lottie ignored her, looking beyond her. Mrs Baker pointed
out the small toilets. Lottie tried one out, urinated, seemed to
take them for granted. She cleared the table systematically;
she took the books off, threw them on the floor, pointed out
the ones she knew; then she fixed the chairs and set out
spoons. Lottie said that they had no dishes. They were
shown to her, but she didn't get them. Miss Wilkins got them.
Then Lottie used them—'pouring' coffee, putting in sugar
and cream. She insisted that her mother sit with straight
legs at the little table. She fed her mother and sometimes
Miss Wilkins. But if Miss Wilkins made advances to her

C

(such as a hug) Lottie did not accept. She noticed the tray of turtles and the fish: "See this, Mommy." Miss Wilkins: "Turtles." Mrs Baker: "Pick one up?" Lottie: "No, they might bite me! They might bite me!" Lottie seemed to enjoy looking at herself in the mirror over the sink. A third teacher came in; Lottie ignored her.

When Mrs Baker said, "Lottie, it is time to go", Lottie paid no attention. Her mother said it again, more forcefully. Then Lottie came quickly and willingly. They went out of the big room to the locker room; Lottie saw the slide, climbed up the steps to the top, talking all the way: "This is not the slide, these are the steps" (describing just what she had to do, over and over). She slid down many times while her mother and Miss Wilkins were talking. Mrs Baker: "O.K., just one more turn." Then Lottie was soon out of the door and running down the hall. Her mother called, "Wait for me." Lottie dashed to the outside door, hung onto the bar, waiting for the push and ride—just as she had done the year before. (Near the end, when another mother and child came in, Lottie darted quickly to her mother.)

Lottie visits nursery school to meet her teachers and see the room. She says before going that she "loves" Miss Wilkins, her teacher. She is in high spirits, examines materials—pointing out, judging—sets up serving-coffee play with her mother and Miss Wilkins. She is wary of advances by Miss Wilkins; she primarily reacts to (and orders about) her mother. She ignores the other two teachers. Lottie is curious about the turtles, then shrinks back from them: "They might bite me!" She uses the small, indoor slide repeatedly with a running verbal account. Lottie dashes to her mother at the entrance of a strange mother and child. On the way out, Lottie repeats the running-down-the-hall and swinging-on-the-door pattern of leaving school from the year before, when she used to call for her older sister Dorrie.

THE FIRST DAY

20 September 1956. Record of first session at nursery school

This was Lottie's first regular day at nursery school. I went in the car with Mrs Baker and Lottie. Lottie was quite happy, saying, "I'm going to dancing school" (reminiscent of the way she calls orange juice apple juice, even though one feels that she knows the correct word).

I went in with Mrs Baker and Lottie, first to the locker room. Lottie walked slowly, grasping her mother firmly. Mrs Baker looked for and found Lottie's locker. Lottie saw the small slide, exclaimed, then climbed right up. Mrs Baker put Lottie's jacket in her locker and suggested that they go into the room. (There were three teachers, five mothers, and five children; most of them were sitting at various tables; a few children were moving around.) Lottie seemed quite hesitant, hanging on to her mother's skirt.

We went in and sat down at a table. There was talk between mothers while Lottie looked around. She got up and took me by the hand over to the turtle tray, saying "rattles, rattles" (turtles) looking for them. A teacher said that another girl was holding them. The teacher put them back into the tray. Lottie watched, clutching my hand tightly. She took me to the sink and watched a boy there, then back to the turtles. "They'll get out!" she said, sounding worried. A turtle was standing on its hind legs in the shallow pan. I assured her that they could not get out and said that she could hold them; but Lottie did not want to. "Pick me up," she said, pulling on my skirt. I picked Lottie up. Miss Wilkins suggested that I observe outside. I brought Lottie back to Mrs Baker and left the room. Lottie sat with her mother at the table; Mrs Baker showed her a book and a puzzle. Mrs Baker introduced Lottie to another girl, Alice. Lottie took one piece of the puzzle, placed it in, took it out, not paying very much attention to it. She was mainly looking around. She watched attentively while a boy at the next table played

23

with a peg-board. He scrambled the pegs and she seemed very interested. Afterwards, she went and put in some pegs.

Lottie saw a boy and his mother go into the bathroom and close the door. She made no comment. A full five minutes later, Lottie said, "Wanna go toidy." Lottie went with her mother. Mrs Baker knocked: "Does Timmy want privacy?" "You may come in." Timmy was on the toilet. Lottie took her pants off, her eyes glued on the boy; she sat on the toilet, but she did not urinate: "Don't have to." When they came out, Lottie made another tour to the sink and the turtles.

Miss Wilkins said it was time for juice and crackers. Many of the children went to watch her get the cups and crackers. Lottie went into the locker room too; she wanted to get down the crackers and cups (but they were up too high). She did help to clean the table off and to put the books away. She took one cracker and asked for another. Apple juice was served. Lottie kept giving her juice to her mother to drink. Then Lottie drank some, too. Lottie was sitting on her mother's lap. There was talk about raincoats and sisters and brothers—between the teacher and the other children. Then Miss Wilkins said: "Now we'll go home. See you next week." Everyone went into the locker room to get coats. Lottie started to go to the slide. But when another child ran to the slide, Lottie stopped and turned back. Miss Wilkins picked her up: "Goodbye." Lottie reared back. Mrs Baker said goodbye. A few minutes later they came back in again (Mrs Baker carrying Lottie) to get a raincoat. Lottie's teachers said goodbye to her once more. This time Lottie said, "Bye, bye", smiling.

Lottie states she is going to "dancing school". (Dancing school is where Dorrie goes, Lottie just visits and watches there.) This misnomer—on the first day of school—which could be merely a minor slip or confusion, is the first indication of a reaction that deepens and develops as attendance at nursery school continues.

Lottie is hesitant, clinging to her mother's skirt when they enter the twos' main room, crowded with children, mothers, and teachers. She takes me on a tour of the room, first to the turtle tray, calling them "rattles". For Lottie—whose verbal ability is particularly well-developed and accurate for her age— a word mix-up of this kind usually denotes ambivalence or some special involvement. The turtles worry Lottie: "They'll get out!" She demands to be picked up when I suggest that she can hold them. Lottie is, in general, a fearless devotee of animals, yet she projects on these small, dark, moist creatures her most aggressive fantasies. When she first set eyes on them, on her visit to school the day before, Lottie cried out that they might bite her. The turtles continue for some time to be the focus of both aggressive fears and, later, aggressive actions.

Lottie follows a boy, after an interval, into the lavatory; she does not urinate, just watches—her eyes glued on him. Before nursery school began, she showed some strong, negative reactions to boys. Apparently, Lottie is beginning to differentiate the sexes. Nursery school, with its half male peer population, its free, mixed toileting and undressing activities, brings boy-girl differences inescapably to the fore. In contrast, Lottie's home has a prevailingly female atmosphere. Lottie helps to clear the table at juice-time. She sits on her mother's lap, giving her juice to her mother and then to herself.

IV

Lottie within her Family

DESCRIPTION

What does Lottie look like? A little person all of one piece; tan and gold—hair, eyes, and skin appear to be matched; heart-shaped face with wide-set eyes, a small nose that disappears at the non-existent bridge, pink cheeks, firm chin with wide-curved mouth; light-brown and gold fine hair parted on the side, caught up with an essential barrette—above all, a mobile face, lit with laughter or shadowed by distress. Lottie appears small yet sturdy, firm and well-formed; she is in the middle range of her age level in height and weight.

She moves quickly, trots rather than walks, with a slightly toed-in gait, legs flinging out below the knee as she goes. In the early fall, Lottie seemed to stumble and fall outdoors, bump into things indoors, more than one would expect of a child who was so competent in the use of both large and small muscles. Perhaps this was because her eyes and mind were so set on the goal, she would cut corners and hurry. Generally, she was not bothered by the bumps and falls (if they were not too hard), picked herself up and continued with the action in view. The goal itself—be it drinking a glass of juice or climbing up the slide—is always executed with more care than getting to it or returning from it.

FAMILY CONSTELLATION

Lottie's parents are in their early thirties, of middle-class, Jewish background. Her father is in professional work on a schedule

26

that brings him in and out of the home at irregular hours. Lottie's mother is in the home at all hours (with infrequent 'days off'). Heidi—the oldest daughter—is ten and a half years old, attends fifth grade from nine to three at the nearby public school, belongs to Girl Scouts, takes ballet and piano lessons. Dorrie, the middle sister of five and three-quarter years, started morning kindergarten this year at the same school as her older sister. Mrs Adams, who comes in to help several afternoons a week, is an important part of the family. Lottie says: "Goody— I love she", when told Mrs Adams is coming today. There is also an assortment of pets: a tiny dog, Popo; a small, much mauled cat; a canary; and a bowlful of guppies—each carefully named by the girls.

The Bakers are a close-knit group. Leisure time is a family affair: a drive to the country, an excursion to the beach, dinner out, or a trip to New York City to visit relatives (perhaps taking in a parade or the zoo)—they pile into the car (including Lottie) and drive off.

On the rare occasions (perhaps once in two or three months) that Mr and Mrs Baker go off by themselves for a day or short weekend, the girls are left in the care of either their grandmother, or Mrs Adams, or myself. Lottie has always accepted these arrangements very well and usually behaves at her best. There is always much talk on Lottie's part about where Mommy went and when she will be home.

When Mr and Mrs Baker go out for the evening, Lottie is always told that they are going and who the sitter (one of a few high-school girls) will be. Most often, Lottie's mother puts her to bed first—if possible, with the sitter there. Lottie announces that she does not like the sitter—no matter who it is—and does not want her. However, she then settles down and sleeps well.

Lottie is not low-man on the totem pole in the Baker family; neither is she the cute, sweet baby. She is a powerful, assertive little person in her own right. Lottie fits in well in this family, which regards each member as a distinct individual, to whom respect and consideration are due for foibles as well as for talents.

27

Lottie's father is the final authority for all basic family decisions. He believes in a balance between freedom for his children for exploring, learning, and growing—and prompt obedience to, and respect for, adult demands. By and large, he elicits just these responses from his children; and, in addition, their love and admiration. Mr Baker's work is in the biological sciences. He is a firm believer in using correct, scientific terminology for the parts of the body and their functions. He talks with his daughters in these terms and, when he considers it appropriate, discusses various biological principles with them.

But the father is at home for only brief, irregular moments of the girls' day. The bulk of the vast detail of the household is handled by the mother. While basically agreeing with Mr Baker, Mrs Baker's approach varies more with the nature of the demands placed upon her and with her own feelings. She is the hub of the wheel: at her best, giving and receiving warmth and consideration, sensitive to needs at each level, taking pride and pleasure in her three girls. In the hurly-burly of the day—clothes, schools, meals, snacks, chauffeuring, lessons, friends, cleaning up, budgeting, laundry, shopping, play—there may be times of exasperation too, when shouting is resorted to, spankings administered. She believes that the girls must accept this as part of herself as a human being. Sometimes—especially after a period of illness in the family, nights without sleep—Mrs Baker is overcome by a feeling of being put upon, pulled in all directions; she desperately needs time to herself, for herself. But these moments pass; primarily she feels satisfaction and fulfillment in her role.

In Lottie's world, her two sisters—Dorrie and Heidi—loom very large. She gives the impression of constantly running very fast to catch up to them. She listens, she watches, she imitates; she must make sure that she always gets *her* turn, as big a piece to eat, and the opportunity to put in *her* 'two cents' on every topic of conversation. In the summer she frequently said, "I can't do that. I too little." That phrase is rare now. She has not been thought of as a baby in the family for over a year. So

28

much so, that when Heidi was recently taken to task for scolding Lottie severely for wetting herself (a rare occurrence) she sheepishly admitted: "I forgot Lottie was only two and a half." Even Lottie's mother claims that she must remind herself constantly that Lottie is only a two-year-old.

The frequent pattern of a less stressful, easier sibling relationship between first and third child (rather than between 'neighbor' siblings) does not apparently hold in the Baker family. Here, rather, Heidi quite early took on (and has maintained) a protective role with Dorrie; and Dorrie, in her turn, has assumed a similar role with Lottie. For Lottie—as her mother says—the sun rises and sets on Dorrie. "Where is Dorrie?" is Lottie's perennial question. When Lottie's mother is not there and anything goes wrong (or if Mrs Baker has punished Lottie), Lottie rushes to Dorrie, flings her arms around her, clings tightly, sobbing "Dorrie, Dorrie!" Dorrie accepts this as to be expected —hugs Lottie in return until she quiets down. Lottie will take more from Dorrie than from anyone else. Dorrie, on her part, gives more care and shows greater sensitivity to Lottie than to anyone else. She has complained lately that Lottie is an "awful copy-cat" (of her)—but she also seems proud of it. Dorrie can be cutting with her sharp, quick intelligence, sometimes ignoring another person's feelings. But with Lottie she is more likely to empathize. Lottie's explicit identification with Dorrie, which developed this fall, is discussed with the nursery-school material.

Heidi, the oldest, is the organizer and creator of many of the games and activities that are sustained, off and on, for months in the family. Artistically gifted, lover of small animals and all tiny things, affectionately dubbed "the nursery-school teacher" (by the adults), she will gather together the "little ones" (any children around younger than she, and sometimes her peers) and have "school" going in the twinkling of an eye. It can be roller-skating school (even if she is a beginner) or "real" school (she even started teaching subtraction to four-year-olds). When Heidi began taking piano lessons this fall, she almost immediately started teaching Dorrie and Lottie, separately. She proudly reported that Lottie could tell the difference between white and black keys and could find middle C. From Heidi has come the passion for "little dolls" (or "littles" as they are called) and "set-ups". A large collection of tiny dolls, animals, dishes, furniture, clothes, bits of material, blocks, and tissues provides the raw material. The set-up is the particular choice of dolls and so forth, organized compactly in a box for the game of the moment. Essentially, it is playing house—with infinite variation. Each child usually has her own independent set-up, although there may be joint play, such as "visiting" back and forth.

Lottie participates fully in all these activities. She is an enthralled student in Heidi's schools. Heidi has said that Lottie plays littles almost as well as Dorrie. She can indeed. She knows all the names, rank order of value, and owners of the several dozen dolls involved. She is as hard a bargainer as any of the girls when it comes to picking and choosing. She can be absorbed for long periods, talking away (as they all do), delicately and expertly arranging the tiny toys. But she can also, in a moment, destroy a set-up with a wild sweep of her arm.

Before Lottie could talk, she uttered a long screech (something between crying and screaming) protesting against anything that was not to her liking. It was loud and piercing. It could not be ignored. In playing with her, both Heidi and Dorrie learned to compromise in such a way that Lottie was satisfied (at least momentarily) and their game could continue. The screech is still used—now combined with words: "Nooooo!" or "My tuuurn!"—and it is still commanding. Lottie is not an easy play-mate; yet she can give a lot of satisfaction with her enthusiasm, her quickness in catching on, and her frank admiration of her older sisters.

Heidi, more easily than Dorrie, can be exasperated by Lottie. And, with an edge to her tone, an over-quickness in handling (more 'teacherish' than teaching), Heidi can set Lottie off into rebellion. But she is also capable of the most expert care of Lottie, through all routines as well as play. Even though Heidi now chooses to spend increasingly more of her free time with friends of her own age, there are always some times of the day when either by choice or by request she is in charge of the little ones.

Mrs Baker feels that Heidi is so much bigger and older, that Lottie regards her almost as an adult; whereas Dorrie is much closer to Lottie—another child—someone, therefore, it is possible for her to model herself after, to strive to be like. Heidi treats Lottie more as Mrs Baker does; but for Dorrie, Lottie is a fellow child.

There is, of course, some bickering, teasing, quarreling, and complaining among the three girls. But, basically, good feeling and strong family loyalty prevail. Both Mr and Mrs Baker come down quickly and sharply on unpleasantness or unfairness between siblings. They expect some of it, but it is not condoned behavior.

THE HOUSE

The Bakers live in a growing New England town, set between two cities. Their house—an old, two-storey, remodeled structure —is on a residential, tree-lined street not far from the center.

They do not use their small front lawn. All activity goes on in the back-yard with its large grassy section and paved driveway, widening and curving around to the separate garage (used mostly for wheel-toy storage and play) and the "way-back"—a fenced-in, grassed area with the large outdoor equipment (swings, teeter-go-round, sandbox) and trees.

The downstairs of the house includes the living room, a large kitchen with a small dining area, and the lavatory. Two stair-cases lead up to the second floor: one from the living room, carpeted, going up to Lottie's and Dorrie's room on one side and Mr and Mrs Baker's room on the other; the second, steep and narrow, leads from the kitchen to Heidi's room and the bathroom. Upstairs there are three bedrooms, a bathroom, and a tiny TV room. Lottie and Dorrie share a bedroom-playroom with two doors—one to the front stairs, one to Heidi's room. Heidi's room is smaller and her second door opens out to the back stairs and bathroom. From the parents' room are doors to

31

the front stairs and the bathroom. It is an interconnected arrangement, making it necessary for Lottie and Dorrie to go through either their parents' or Heidi's room to get to the bathroom. The circular house-plan makes for great sport, too—racing round and round the second floor, or going down one staircase and up the other.

EARLIER HISTORY

Mrs Baker reviewed (25 November 1956) some of the weaning and toilet-training history of Lottie. Lottie was nursed for about five months, then weaned to the bottle. She made this transition very easily even though Mrs Baker had used bottles rarely. Lottie loved the bottle and drank large quantities of milk. At about thirteen or fourteen months she was weaned from the bottle to the cup. Although Lottie was then drinking juice very competently and happily from a cup or glass, she refused persistently to drink milk from a cup. Mrs Baker does not remember that Lottie showed any other disturbance at the time. Mrs Baker handled the absence of milk drinking by adding milk to Lottie's food—cereal, potatoes, junket, ice cream, cottage cheese—anything that could absorb added milk or that contained milk. The refusal to drink milk lasted many months. In the last six months Lottie has been drinking more milk, although fruit juices are still her primary drink; she will drink one-third to one-half of a glass at a meal, especially when her sisters are also drinking and if flavoring and coloring straws are supplied.

Mrs Baker did nothing about toilet training until early last spring when Lottie was about twenty-one months old. Then she sat Lottie on a toilet-seat now and then, unsystematically, with occasional urinary success. Mrs Baker said that she was really waiting for warm weather so that she could put Lottie in pants and dresses instead of diapers. The occasional attempts with scattered success (only for urinating) continued until early June. Then, within one week (right after Lottie's second birthday), Lottie, her mother says, completely "trained herself". She urinated and defecated only on the toilet and became dry at night.

Since June she has maintained sphincter control with hardly a lapse. Lottie can use the toilet efficiently by herself; sometimes she asks her mother to go with her. She uses the regular toilet without any special seat and also has in her room (particularly for early morning use) a small toidy-chair.

Ever since Lottie started to use the toilet she has made frequent comments about the possibility, or lack of probability, of her falling in. Mrs Baker feels that this has not represented any deep-seated fear on Lottie's part, but rather a small degree of anxiety which she has handled successfully for herself with a lot of talk about it and, sometimes, a game of letting herself down into the toilet and then pulling herself out: "I fall into the toidy? I not fall in. I too big!" She has also been very interested in flushing the toilet, insisting on doing it herself and watching it to the end.

V

Autumn

"I don't like my own self."

From 20 September to 18 December 1956 Lottie attended twenty-two sessions of nursery school. She missed one day because of a cold. During these first three months of nursery school, a poignant drama unfolded with unexpected twists and turns. It is surprising when one considers that the central character was a little girl of two years and three months, normal, well-developed, highly verbal, apparently ready for nursery school; that the school was one of the best, with an individually oriented policy of handling adjustment to school by having the mother present as long as needed; and that the program for the twelve two-year-olds in the group involved only two mornings a week of two and a half hours each.

SEPARATION FROM MOTHER

On the way to the first day of school Lottie announced that she was going to a place that her sister Dorrie attended (dancing school). This small remark prefigured Lottie's major means of coping with school and separation from her mother: identification with her five-year-old sister.

During the second session Lottie inadvertently calls her teacher "Miss Peters". (Miss Peters was Dorrie's teacher the year before.) She immediately catches her own slip, and laughingly says to her mother, "Not Miss Peters!" Going outdoors, she asks Miss Wilkins if they will "see the bunny outside". (The spring before, Dorrie's class at nursery school had rabbits in their yard.) When Miss Wilkins explains that they do not have any bunnies now, Lottie persists: "Wanna see where the no bunnies is."

Driving to school for the third session, Lottie says she is going to see her teachers, Miss Wilkins and Mrs Zerber, and her friends. She adds, smiling, "I hate my friends." She brings to school, and leaves there, her doll "Honeybunch" (which she later indicates, in 7,[1] represents Dorrie). When her mother leaves her for the first time to repark the car, Lottie runs to the locker room and stands by her locker, calling out over and over, laughing: "Mommy! Daddy! Dorrie! Heidi!" Mrs Baker returns after ten minutes, finds Lottie on Miss Wilkins's lap, and Lottie turns briefly away from her mother.

At home (3-4) Lottie says to her mother: "Say, 'I don't like my own self.'" Her mother answers: "But I do." Lottie insists: "Say, 'I don't like my own self.' It's a game!" Lately, her mother reports, Lottie has been frequently saying "I don't like my own self." When her mother asks, "Who are we going to see at nursery school?" Lottie replies, "Somebody real—nobody."

Lottie insists on wearing a skirt like Dorrie's on the fifth morning. On the drive to school she says, "I love Wilkins." She asks again about Dorrie's teacher the previous year: "Miss Peters not there? Where is she?" In a conversation with Miss Wilkins at juice-time, Lottie announces that Dorrie is at kindergarten. When Miss Wilkins agrees and adds that Lottie is at nursery school, Lottie protests: "No, Lottie's at kindergarten too!"

---

[1] The fifty-one nursery-school sessions which Lottie attended during the year are numbered in chronological order. They are always referred to by these numbers, which sometimes appear in parentheses. The exact date of each school session is shown in Appendix A.

In order to avoid giving the date for every home observation, its time-point is designated in terms of the nursery-school sessions. For example, '(7-8)' means that the behavior described occurred on a day between the seventh and eighth school sessions; '(before 7)' means that the behavior described took place before school on the day of the seventh session; '(after 7)' means after school on the day of the seventh session.

35

Thus, by the fifth session, dressed in a skirt like Dorrie's (well-armoured in her identification with her sister), Lottie could bound into school in high spirits and, later, grandly tell her mother to go off. As they enter the yard, Lottie says to Mrs Baker: "You go bye-bye own self." But this is probably the highest level of success she could achieve by identification: 'I am not small, frightened Lottie going to nursery school—I am big, strong Dorrie going to kindergarten.' Nevertheless, if she could not cope with nursery school as her own small self (at home she was going around saying that she didn't like her own self), perhaps the shield of 'being Dorrie', even at the cost of denying herself, was a necessary defense during the first difficult period at school to enable her slowly to get used to the strange horde of children, the unfamiliar room, the different ways and routines of doing things; perhaps it made it possible for a relationship of trust to start between herself and her teacher, so that eventually she could relinquish her mother in school.

Lottie bounces in blithely for the seventh session, bringing her doll "Crying" from home and announcing to Miss Wilkins: "This is the sister of Honeybunch and of Dorrie." Using this equation, Honeybunch represents Dorrie and Crying is the stand-in for Lottie. Honeybunch has been left in the office. Lottie asks about her every so often, has gone to see her in the office, and wants her left there. Thus there is a doll-surrogate of her sister Dorrie in the nursery-school office, and now one of Lottie herself at school in her room.

At home (8–9) Mrs Baker tells Lottie that they will call for Dorrie at school. "We going to get Dorrie at nursery school?" Lottie asks. Her ambivalence to school is still manifest: she says "I love nursery school" in the car on the way to the eleventh session, and then at the door of her room, quietly, "I hate nursery school."

Lottie has three "good" mornings at school (11, 12, and 13) in which she can accept her mother leaving for increasing periods. Then, at home before the fourteenth session of school, Lottie states openly and seriously her identification with her sister:

36

LOTTIE   I'm Dorrie. Call me Dorrie.

MRS BAKER   No, you're my little girl Lottie and you're going to your nursery school today. You can pretend whatever you want, but I can't play that game with you.

In school (14) Lottie undergoes the longest separation yet from her mother; on her return, Lottie engages in the most unruly and demanding behavior thus far. For forty minutes she pulls and tugs at Mrs Baker, dumps and throws toys, frequently looking up at her mother and smiling. On her way out, she has a conversation with her teacher:

LOTTIE   I'm Dorrie and I want my picture to take home. I will hang it right under Dorrie's.

MISS WILKINS You're *Lottie* and it's a fine picture. You may take it home and hang it wherever you like.

It is as if Lottie were already giving up her defensive identification with her sister when she states it in words and lays it open to reality and its inevitable rejection by her mother and teacher. Then, if Lottie can no longer 'be' her five-year-old sister Dorrie in school, she becomes herself, a two-year-old, disturbed and angry with this new school experience and with her mother for leaving her there.

During the next three nursery-school sessions (15, 16, and 17) Lottie objects more strongly to her mother leaving and tends to cry for her at the transition time between indoor and outdoor play. Perhaps when Lottie goes to her locker for her outdoor clothes—the first stop in the morning after coming from home with her mother and the last stop at the end of school before leaving for home—her longing for her mother is intensified. This is the first breakthrough of her feelings in crying and immediately precedes the more complete release in the eighteenth session. Lottie is more clinging and demanding when her mother returns. Nevertheless, Mrs Baker is able to absent herself for about half the morning each time.

D

Mrs Baker reports that Lottie was "impossible" in the morning at home on the day before 18; she followed her mother around everywhere, holding on to her, constantly underfoot. Lottie's older sister Heidi describes breakfast that same morning: "All Lottie does is to copy Dorrie! She looks at her all the time and whatever she sees Dorrie do, she does. When Dorrie moves her napkin, Lottie does too."

On the eighteenth day of nursery school Lottie bursts into tears when her mother says goodbye. She cries hard for the first time in school, her face hot and flushed. It is now two months since school began. When Mrs Baker returns, one hour later, Lottie dashes over to her with a big smile, and plays freely ("as if Lottie felt released") at her mother's side. Lottie gets her own two dolls which were left at school, Honeybunch and Crying. While she is playing with them she says to Mrs Baker: "This is not Dorrie's school. This is Lottie's school." She takes both dolls home with her and she switches their surrogate names: large Honeybunch is now Lottie and little Crying is now Dorrie.

Perhaps Lottie no longer needs to have with her the Crying doll as Lottie because she herself can accept the school situation as it is and can express her feelings for the first time, crying hard when her mother leaves her.

The period of denial defense seems to be drawing to a close and with its termination comes the eruption of surface disturbance. When Lottie renounces her denial defense she is left vulnerable to the full impact of separation anxiety. Instead of the steady improvement that her mother anticipated with Lottie's acknowledgement of nursery school as her own, Lottie's behavior deteriorates. She cannot let her mother leave at all; she cries bitterly when her mother does go; she clings more and more to her mother in school, less able to play independently than before; her play is limited, regressed, uncontrolled and violent at times; she loses urinary control at home, in token fashion (a few minor accidents), for the first time after being completely dry for half a year. Mrs Baker is so discouraged that she seriously considers the possibility of withdrawing Lottie from nursery school for a time.

38

During these first three months of school, from the end of September to the end of December, several secondary themes can be discerned within the principal one of Lottie's working out her own self-feelings and separation from her mother in school.

RELATIONSHIP WITH TEACHER

Lottie gradually accepts and becomes attached to her main teacher Miss Wilkins and, to a lesser extent, to Mrs Zerber the assistant teacher. (There are also one or two assistant teachers who change every six weeks.) During 3, Lottie hugs Mrs Zerber and she is on Miss Wilkins's lap when her mother returns from her first short absence. But Lottie's mixed and changing attitudes are revealed in 4. She wants her mother, *not* the teacher, to help her at a time when Mrs Baker is assisting another child. She goes to Miss Wilkins to be picked up when her teacher is comforting a boy crying for his mother. Lottie brings her doll to Miss Wilkins to be dressed and afterwards throws the blanket her teacher has wrapped around it to the floor. Miss Wilkins has another child on her lap in the sandbox and Lottie goes on her lap with the other child. She is especially drawn to her teacher when she is mothering other children. Before school (5 and 6) Lottie says, "I love Wilkins." During 9, Mrs Baker refuses to have Lottie on her lap; Lottie then accepts Miss Wilkins's offer to sit on her lap. Later, when she is very tired, Lottie flings herself into Miss Wilkins's arms.

Though there is little material from the next eight sessions on Lottie's direct interaction with her teacher, it is clear that Lottie is accepting her care more and more during the increasing separations from her mother. The day (18) when Lottie cries hard for the first time when her mother leaves, she stays very close to Miss Wilkins during Mrs Baker's absence. And she goes right on her teacher's lap when her mother leaves briefly for a second time, later that same morning.

However, Lottie is almost entirely absorbed in her mother

during the last four nursery-school sessions before the Christmas vacation (19, 20, 21, 22). She hovers near her mother during a good part of 21. Then, after another mother leaves, promising a present, Lottie tells Mrs Baker to go and bring *her* a present. In 22, Lottie permits Mrs Baker to go to make several telephone calls, but she waits in the same spot for her return. When Mrs Baker asks Lottie to get down off her lap and sit in a chair beside her, Lottie gets down and throws the nearby chairs to the floor. She does not go to her teacher. But she stays indoors with Miss Wilkins and a few children during the outdoor playtime, with Mrs Baker in the room. Lottie appears to be content to be with Miss Wilkins, ordering her about (to play the piano), reminiscent of the way she sometimes commands her mother at home.

RELATIONSHIP WITH MOTHER AT HOME

Separation from the mother at home is a very different matter. Surrounded by people and objects close and familiar to her, occupied with the usual, everyday activities and routines, Lottie can manage quite well. She has experienced occasional, short home separations since infancy. She does not resort at home to the intricate, defensive maneuvers that are set in motion by being left by her mother at nursery school. And yet there is no doubt that her mother is almost constantly on her mind. There are also indications that, over this period of difficulty in separating from her mother in school, Lottie shows increasing intensity of longing for her mother during home separations.

I am putting Lottie to bed (after 6) while her mother is out for the evening. Lottie doesn't want to be helped: "do it self", she insists. Everything must be done just so, in the precise sequence and manner that her mother and she use. After she has just urinated on her toidy-chair, out of the usual order, Lottie insists on going again a few minutes later, in the 'correct' sequence. She knows where everything is, how everything is to be done. With great effort, she manages to reach back for the toilet paper while still sitting on the toilet and carefully wipes herself: "Mommy told me to." At the sink she replaces the toothbrush in the holder, remarking that Mommy's is next to hers, Daddy's across the way—and with a wide, embracing gesture she says lovingly: "Mommy's next to mine!" Then, after the clothes are arranged properly, the correct nightlight is on, and the songs sung, Lottie goes off to sleep. To be very good, to do everything just as she does with Mother (even, rather, just as Mother would want her to do), serves to keep Mother in the forefront—almost as if she were really there—and, perhaps, magically to bring Mother back safely.

There is a great deal of talk and joking by Lottie with me (13-14) about where her mother has gone. Lottie hears the familiar sounds of an adult coming into the house—footsteps up the back steps, the slam of the door—her father appears and Lottie bursts out, "I thought it was *Mommy!*" Two weeks later, Mrs Baker is on the telephone arranging for a sitter (15-16) and Lottie interrupts: "I don't want Karen. I want Daddy to sit for me." Mrs Baker is ill a few days after (16-17), but Lottie insists that she get up to dress her. At my house for the day, Lottie asks frequently about her mother. When she finds Mrs Baker in the kitchen on her return home she says with great surprise, "You waked up, Mommy!" Mrs Baker goes shopping in the afternoon (the day after 22); Lottie talks frequently about her mother and she keeps asking: "When will Mommy come back?" By the end of the afternoon Lottie is on the chair by the window, peering out at the driveway, watching and waiting for her mother's return.

During the autumn Lottie shows increasing resistance to outright restrictions; they seem sometimes to goad her to tenacious insistence on the forbidden act or object. She is extremely well-informed and clear for her age about the rules and regulations of her world. By and large, she is cooperative and reliable about daily routines, play, and safety. But every so often she picks an opening for guerilla warfare against authority, and proceeds to assert her will with a power felt by those around her to be quite

41

out of proportion to her size, age, and condition in life. Lottie is indeed surrounded by quite a collection of authority figures. Foremost is her mother—with her father more dimly, but even more powerfully, set above. Then come her sisters, followed by my family. Finally, there are other friends of her sisters who occasionally function in an authority role for Lottie. Lottie usually chooses side issues over which to wage her battles—often, during this first period of school, in the food area: she insists on something to eat ("bigger" than allowed) when it is not permitted, while refusing to eat at the acceptable times. Later in the year, what to wear becomes another favored battleground.

In school (13) she demands a big cookie. Refusing the offer of a small piece, she persists and gets her way. Then, having won the skirmish, she graciously breaks off part of the plunder and returns it to the box. Playing outdoors at home with a large group of children (17-18) Lottie persists in climbing up the unsafe cellar doors. After having to be carried off them by her mother, she lies on the top step with the tips of her toes touching the forbidden doors—a token victory.

Sometimes, caught up in a struggle, Lottie is capable of re-structuring and solving the problem in her own way. Lottie and her mother are playing together (13-14) with Dorrie's small stuffed kangaroo with a baby in its pouch. Lottie is very insistent about wanting to detach the baby, despite Mrs Baker's demon-stration that it is sewn on and might come apart if removed. Finally Lottie agrees to let it stay: "The mommy doesn't want the baby to get lost," she says. A few weeks later (19-20) Mrs Baker spanks Lottie for being very wild. Lottie doesn't cry—she sits still and tight. Then she grabs me in a hug and says, almost in tears, "I want Mommy to read me a book before my nap." When her mother agrees, she recovers her good spirits.

After six weeks of nursery school (through the fourteenth session) Mrs Baker reports that she does not notice any particular differences between school and non-school days in Lottie's be-havior at home. Lottie, she says, acts out her feelings about school primarily at the time in school, and she does not carry them over to the home. However, a month later (after 22) Mrs Baker feels that Lottie is fighting her both at home and at school. She wonders whether to take Lottie out of school for a while, if there is no improvement after the vacation.

For the first third of the year in nursery school Lottie is primarily involved with two adults, her mother and her teacher Miss Wilkins. She is both very aware and wary of the children in her group. Most of Lottie's activities that do not include adults are carried out by herself, alone. This keeping apart from her peers contrasts sharply with Lottie's warm response to both an older and a younger child in the school situation.

On the way to school for the third session, Lottie remarks: "I'm going to see my friends. I hate my friends." During 4, with her mother's help and direction, Lottie engages in her first joint play—building with large blocks with a boy. Also, she pushes for her turn on the slide. Outdoors, Lottie cries when a boy sweeps sand in her eyes and is comforted by her mother. It is noteworthy that Lottie reacts with intense laughter to a boy's crying at his mother's departure (7) at a time when her own mother is present. This is one of the indications for what seems to be Lottie's secondary denial defense—pseudo-elation—which will be discussed in a later section.

Lottie is happy and gay (after 5 and 9), picking up four-year-old Jean, in the oldest group's room next door, to take her home. (She knows Jean from Dorrie's dancing class.) Lottie shows delight in a younger child, the sister of one of her own classmates, who visits school during the seventh session.

Lottie seems not to be so affected by all the crying among other children in school in 11. But later that day, at home, she tells Caron's father about school; the account is almost entirely about children crying. Outdoors, during 16, Lottie plays in the pebble patch with several other children—they throw pebbles at one another. At music-time in 21, Lottie wants to have a drum

43

a boy is using. When it turns out that he brought the drum from home and cannot give it up, Lottie, who had been waiting (impatiently) for a turn at the suggestion of her mother, is unappeased by the offer of a substitute. She makes a remark to her mother implying that Mrs Baker has betrayed her.

At home during this first period of school Lottie is closely involved with her two sisters and their friends. She continues to be an excited, eager participant in their activities. More than ever she imitates her sister Dorrie. An incident in which Lottie inadvertently hurts a friend reveals her capacity for empathy with another child.

Lottie joins Heidi and Kaye upstairs (15-16); they tease her and she screams and shouts, "Noooo!" But when she complains and Mrs Baker suggests that she stay downstairs, Lottie goes right back up to them. They all come down to the kitchen where Heidi and Kaye grab something to eat and offer Lottie a half slice of bread. Lottie refuses: "I want a big one!" After all the talk explaining why she cannot have it, she insists again: "I want a big one!" Lottie roller-skates for the first time, with joy and competence, at my house (16-17). Caron gives Lottie her beginner roller skates and ice skates. Lottie says: "Not for Dorrie. Just for *me*!" On the day before the eighteenth session, Lottie happily roller-skates in her yard in the midst of a group of nine children up to the age of ten, all on skates. She looks up at an airplane flying by and asks, "Who is in that airplane?" When she realizes that all the visiting children have gone, that only Dorrie and Caron are left skating, she remarks, "Nobody is there." A few days later Dorrie teases Lottie, calling her a "naughty girl" (19-20). Mrs Baker tells Dorrie to stop or she cannot go to Caron's house. Lottie rushes in to her mother a few minutes later: "Dorrie can't go. She teased again!" Lottie is napping at home in my care while her mother is out shopping on the day after 22. She cries very hard—"I heard a siren!"—asks for Dorrie, who soothes her, and then she goes off to sleep.

Lottie sweeps her arm across the kitchen counter at home, knocking off a container which accidently hits Caron on the forehead, causing a welt (15-16). Caron cries and I comfort her. A band-aid is applied. Lottie tries very hard to put her arms around Caron, but Caron rejects her advances, finally accepting only one hug. Eight days later, at the same spot in the kitchen, Lottie dashes over to Caron, hugs her and asks, "Where is your band-aid?" When Caron trips on the stairs in Lottie's house a week later (19-20), falls and cries, Lottie laughs in a tense fashion: "Caron pushes me away when I hug her." At two and a half years, Lottie seems to be unusually sensitive to the distress and feelings of another child. She wants to make restitution and she succeeds, a week later. Her memory is very long for her age; over two weeks after the first incident—in a similar situation— she wants to hug, to console again. But remembering, she holds back, verbalizing clearly how her friend would behave if she, Lottie, followed her wish.

ACTIVITIES AND PLAY

School is not for 'learning' for Lottie during these first months, not in the sense of mastery of new skills or using new materials and equipment. Bound up as she is in working through the separation from her mother, developing her relationship with her teachers, and becoming accustomed to the peer group, she is not at liberty within herself to explore or to play freely very much at school.

Activities and objects are not so often interesting to Lottie in themselves; they frequently acquire value because of their connection with people to whom she is closely attached. Thus, at home Lottie continues to play actively and achieve new mastery —stimulated by and emulating her sisters and their friends— apparently unaffected by her experiences at school. Heidi gives her "piano lessons" (after 15); Caron presents her with roller skates and she promptly becomes proficient (16-17), happily joining a large group of skaters a few days later in her yard; she works hard at home mastering her own bolt and screw-nut toy which has also been available at school (but not handled by her there),

45

and she is able to identify almost all the colors of the nuts; Mrs Baker reports that Lottie says the alphabet and counts to thirteen; Lottie plays, delicately and concentratedly, with Caron's tiny precious toys (19-20).

At school Lottie's activities and play are tightly enmeshed in the course of the separation drama enacted with her mother. From the beginning, Lottie is better outdoors; she is more active, freer, and more varied in her play—sandbox, pebble patch, and climbing—all are absorbing (2,3,4,6,13,15,16). She can tell her mother to leave at the start of outdoor play in 5. She stays outside with Mrs Zerber in the following session when her mother goes indoors. In 16, there is the only reported spontaneous, semi-aggressive, and enjoyable play with several other children—the stone throwing in the pebble patch. But it is in this session and the next that Lottie first cries for her mother in school at the transition time between indoors and outdoors. Moreover, after 18, having accepted verbally being 'Lottie in nursery school', she stops going outdoors. She chooses to stay indoors during 20 and 22, even though her mother would accompany her to the yard. There, in the schoolroom, she is Lottie at her worst—in destructive and clinging 'play' expressing her feelings against her mother.

In her dealings with school's small animals, Lottie reveals even more clearly her angry feelings. The "rattles" that frightened her on her first visit to school because "they might bite" become the target of increasing aggression. She throws stones on the turtles (4), picks one up and drops it in her mother's hand. She calls the turtles by their right name by the seventh session. She hurls things into the fishbowl in 8. In the next session there is frenzied play with the turtles, pelting and thumping them. They are not mentioned again until 15 when Mrs Baker reports that Lottie is violent with them, tossing them from pan to pan. The two hamsters are introduced on the following morning of school. Lottie is so intrigued by them that she is diverted from her refusal to let her mother leave. She says goodbye easily while gleefully holding a hamster. (The turtles do not reappear in the school

46

reports.) Lottie's feelings are mixed toward these soft, furry creatures. She delights in them; she cannot keep her hands off them; nevertheless, she cannot restrain her roughness with them. Miss Wilkins remarks (18) that Lottie has been "taking it out on the hamsters". But during the last four sessions of autumn, while Lottie is taking it out directly on her mother, the school's animals are given a respite—there is no further mention of them.

One more animal plays a role for Lottie in school. On the morning of 21 she does not want to go to school, but she is transformed when reminded that she can take her cat that day. She is very possessive about her cat at first. However, she is finally prevailed upon to share it with the other children. Actually the twenty-first is the best of the last four sessions before the vacation which are so discouraging to Mrs Baker. Despite the fact that Lottie is curiously blank and disaffected when her favorite home book is read and her favorite record played, and that she stays close to her mother, scribbling on her list, climbing on her lap, she does send her mother off to get her a present, and she does join the dancing at the end, even after not getting a turn with the drum which she so desperately wants. She also plays with beads in this session, and with the bolt and screw-nut toy that she mastered at home a week before.

Painting is the major new activity for Lottie at nursery school. It is not available at home. She asks for it in 9 and she is radiant when Miss Wilkins promises it for next time. Painting is the highlight of 10. She is absorbed in it in 11, "to show Dorrie". At the end of the fourteenth session, she demands her painting, saying she is Dorrie. It may be significant that, during the two weeks (10 through 14) that she is painting in school, the small animals do not come up in the school reports. Perhaps painting functions as a more grown-up, Dorrie-like activity for Lottie. Paintings by Lottie's sisters are up on the walls at home. There is no doubt that Lottie enjoys participating in this satisfying state of affairs; trying to 'be Dorrie' makes it all the more important. To have something to show from nursery school, not just to tell about juice and crackers, can be very rewarding. The girls do respond at home; they see all kinds of things in the paintings (14-15). However, even though Lottie seems to enjoy painting for its own sake and has so many reasons to continue, she stops temporarily when she stops 'being Dorrie'. It takes several sessions before she can go back to it as Lottie.

Lottie sets in motion a busy traffic of objects between home and school. In the beginning it is one-way—from home. She takes the doll Honeybunch to school on the third morning and leaves her there. She asks for and plays with Honeybunch in the next session. She cannot decide (before 5) whether to take little dolls or a book; she takes the former. But when she enters school and finds Miss Wilkins reading to the children, she cries out that she forgot the book. By 6, she insists on taking something home from school, finally settling for some cracker crumbs. Her doll Crying is brought to school and left there in the seventh session. Although she decides to leave Crying in school at the end of the following morning, in the car going home she exclaims, "We forgot Crying!" By the tenth session, Mrs Baker reports, Lottie always brings a cracker home from school. Of course, she has her paintings to bring back with her (10, 11, 14). She finds and plays with Crying in 15. Both dolls from home assist at the important announcement of the eighteenth session; thereupon, she returns them to her house. Finally, only the plan for taking her cat to visit school enables her to go willingly for the twenty-first session. Perhaps Lottie is trying to break down some of the boundaries between home and school by transferring things back and forth.

Lottie's manipulation of her dolls seems to take part, through projection, in the development and disintegration of her autumn denial defenses. She brings the Dorrie-doll into school to guard her just as she protects herself by identifying with her sister. She places the Crying-Lottie-doll in the schoolroom during the time she denies her need to cry. The same morning on which she cries for the first time when her mother leaves, and also affirms school to be hers during play with the dolls, is their final day at school.

48

FEARS

At school, Lottie's original fear of the turtles biting *her* (visit and first session) is transformed into active aggression against *them* (4, 9, 15). The only other specific fear she shows is in using the toilets: "I won't fall in", she keeps on commenting, rather matter-of-factly, when she goes to the lavatory accompanied by her mother (4, 5, 9). The toilets are smaller than at home, but the flushing is much more powerful and louder. There have been many remarks at home, too, about not falling into the toilet. But it seems to be more of a constant concern at school. Whether it is the rushing water going down, evoking the frightening possibility of being flushed away; or the little boys she sees undressed there, evoking anxious thoughts about an organ she does not possess—the fear is not in any case strong enough to hinder her from going independently to the toilet by the ninth session.

Lottie is very afraid of sirens at home. Fire engines, ambulances, and police cars speed frequently by her house with sirens screaming. This fear developed some months before, and continues throughout, the first period at school. She usually cries hard and must be soothed. But sometimes she attempts to deny her fear. One night when she hears a siren (13-14) Lottie gets out of bed and goes to her older sister's room "to tell *Heidi* not to worry; it was *loud*". Her mother is away when Lottie is frightened by a siren at naptime (after 22); before she can fall asleep, she needs Dorrie as well as me to comfort her. Lottie is sick in bed on the following day, conversing with Dorrie and me:

LOTTIE   I don't cry when I hear a fire engine. Dorrie, do you?
DORRIE   No. When I was little, I thought the firemen *made* the fires.
LOTTIE   If I put my finger in a fire, it would get *burnt*!

Perhaps the fear originated in an early reaction to the piercing, alarming sound (the Baker family moved to their present home

49

when Lottie was two weeks old—Lottie has acute and sensitive hearing) and, later, punitive fantasies of body damage became attached to the earlier fear.

TOILETING

This has never been an area of either pressure or difficulty for Lottie. She trained herself quickly and completely shortly after her second birthday in June 1956, with hardly a lapse since that time.

Lottie is in general casual and competent in toileting both at school and at home. Only her regular comment about not falling in reveals the presence of some slight anxiety. She goes to the lavatory with her mother frequently during the early sessions of school. In the fifth session, she sits at juice-time singing over and over, laughing: "Clothes on the washline. Dry up. You said a mouthful. Dry up." She drinks a large amount of juice and manages to use the toilet four times. This is the morning that she tells her mother to leave. On Mrs Baker's return, Lottie comes up to her cheerfully and says, "I want to go toidy." On her second trip to the lavatory of the ninth session, Lottie goes by herself and is praised by Miss Wilkins. Presumably, from this time on, Lottie continues to use the toilet independently at school.

At home Lottie tries particularly hard when Mrs Baker is away to do exactly as her mother has said about toileting. She is precise about toilet terms and also enjoys toilet-talk play. When Lottie is trying to be especially good while her mother is out for the evening (after 6) she makes sure that she uses the toilet with impeccable form. A month later (13-14) I am taking care of Lottie while Mrs Baker is out of town for the day. In the bathroom I say "Mmm, good" when Lottie urinates. Lottie laughs at me: "Why do you say 'Mmm, good'? That's not cake, it's pee-pee!" Lottie is told about a dog named Bambi (15-16). She shouts, "B-M! B-M!" I say, "Not B-M. *Bambi*." Lottie, laughing, "B-M-bi! B-M-bi!"

It is curious that wetting should be the one slight instance of

regression *at home* during the period that Lottie is actively expressing her aggressive feelings against her mother in school. For
about six weeks Lottie has been occasionally getting her pants
slightly wet by not pulling them down far enough when she
urinates on the small toidy-chair in her room. Mrs Baker thinks
it is probably deliberate on Lottie's part, but she handles it without much comment, merely changing the pants. Then, on the
day after the twentieth session, Mrs Baker hears Heidi loudly
scolding Lottie: "You naughty girl! Why didn't you go to the
toidy on time?" Lottie has urinated on the floor. Mrs Baker is
angry with Heidi for the way she handled Lottie, telling Heidi:
"It was an accident, Lottie has been perfect, she's only two and a
half; obviously, Lottie had played too long and then couldn't get
to the toilet on time." But only a few days later there is a similar
accident. Then again at my house, in the afternoon after the last
day of school before the Christmas vacation, Lottie wets her
pants—a tiny bit—and rushes over to her mother: "I'm wet!"
But she manages to hold in the rest of the urine completely until
she gets to the toilet. Immediately, Lottie has to 'undo' her relapse.
No extra pants being available, she must hang the barely wet
ones over the radiator, insisting that they be absolutely dry
before putting them on.

This is certainly a most controlled loss of control. It may be
that Lottie has witnessed similar lapses at school—not all of her
classmates are toilet-trained—and she is now experimenting at
home. But it is probable that Lottie is also trying to get back at
her mother, choosing, so to speak, a highly safe means of becoming like a baby that she can turn on and off at will. Perhaps she is
'saying', in effect, to her mother: 'You do not love me because
you leave me at school. Therefore, I will not be good, which I
have done out of love for you.' But her mother is not in the least
perturbed by Lottie's wetting. She feels that a few accidents in a
two-year-old are to be expected and she handles them in a matter-
of-fact way. After three attempts, there is only one more instance
of wetting due to loss of control: it occurs at school, in the winter
period.

FOOD AND DRINK

Juice-time is the most positive part of school for Lottie from the beginning. It is conceptualized by her as a snack—not a meal, with urging to eat what you are supposed to—but a pleasurable, free-choice activity.

Lottie achieves a stable independence from her mother in school more quickly in this area than in any other. From 'oneness' with her mother on the first day of school, she moves steadily on to autonomy at juice-time by the fifth session. Although she helps Miss Wilkins to get the table ready and takes two crackers herself on the first day of school, she is on Mrs Baker's lap and keeps giving her mother the juice to drink before she drinks it herself. In the next session (2) she asks her mother for juice and requires Mrs Baker to go with her to ask Miss Wilkins for it. Lottie also insists on her mother sitting in a little chair next to her. Then Lottie falls off her chair and with boisterous laughter does it three times over. After this clowning she eats and drinks, at ease. Lottie asks for crackers in 4, and her mother gives her one. Lottie: "No, let *me* have the basket." Miss Wilkins says that she can pass it and Lottie distributes crackers to the other children. She takes an extra cracker afterwards, which she finally gives to her mother to eat. In the following session (5) Lottie wants Mrs Baker to sit in a small chair before juice-time, which she refuses to do; Lottie goes off to the fishbowl. Nevertheless, she helps Miss Wilkins to clear the table for juice, and then accompanies her copious drinking with song and laughter.

Lottie does not involve her mother again at juice-time except in the eighth session. On this morning one of the girls screams, loud and long, for her mother; Lottie says that she wants to go home. But a moment later she changes her mind: "I think I'll have juice and crackers first." The girl continues to cry and Lottie includes Mrs Baker in this juice-time, making sure she is there. After this, Lottie manages without her mother. Mrs Baker is away from school during juice and crackers for eight school mornings (from 11 through 18). Even during the last four sessions, although Lottie exacts her mother's close presence, she maintains her juice-time independence. In 20, she turns to her mother during juice and says, "I'm restless." The phonograph is brought out for the first time in the next session; chairs are drawn up and the children wait eagerly. But Lottie sits apart with the empty pretzel box in her lap, licking up crumbs of salt, coughing from it, and not showing any overt interest in this favorite home pastime of hers. When Lottie is crawling on her mother's lap during 22 and Mrs Baker tells her that they had better go home if this is all she wants to do at school, Lottie says: "Juice and crackers!" Moreover, Lottie is able to leave her mother to go with Miss Wilkins and three other children on an excursion out of the room to get some pretzels.

Lottie consumes a great quantity of juice and crackers. With most of the other children, she also pushes hard on the boundary of mid-morning juice until by the tenth session, Mrs Baker reports, all the children are eating regularly after juice-time and, by 13, Miss Wilkins is now giving crackers on demand during the second part of the morning, and the demand is tremendous.

When Lottie is determined to take something home from school at the end of the sixth morning, she settles for cracker crumbs. Although she keeps trying to take different things from school that are not allowed to leave the building, crackers are an acceptable alternative and they become her daily exit door-prize by the tenth session.

Lottie's demand for "a big one" both at school and at home seems to be for bigness' sake rather than from oral greediness. She will quickly throw away the whole big gum she has just demanded from her mother, because she does not really like it (3-4). Lottie does return of her own accord, as previously noted, part of the big cracker she has pressed Miss Wilkins to give her in 13. Perhaps being given a large—instead of a two-year-old size—piece of food is a longed-for confirmation of Lottie's urgent wish to be big like her sisters.

To the question by her sisters: "What did you do in school today?" comes Lottie's invariable answer: "Juice and crackers!"

E   53

This is just about all she has to say about school at home until the advent of painting in the tenth session.

At home, Lottie's food pattern of scanty eating at meals along with large snacking apparently consolidates over the first months at school. This may be another way in which Lottie is saying 'no' to her mother at home, perhaps, in part, retaliating for the separation suffering at school. Lottie is particular and vehement about her diet. Actually, she does not imitate either of her sisters in her strong likes and dislikes. She takes after her mother, rather than any other member of the family, in preferring fruity, sour, and salty things. The few mealtime foods that she consistently enjoys are limited to cold cereal for breakfast, bacon for lunch, and some meats for dinner. But orange juice is Lottie's personal nectar. It is her most preferred refreshment, drunk in very large quantity. Curiously, she always calls orange juice "apple juice". Apple juice, which she likes very well, is also called "apple juice". Mrs Baker jokingly says that orange juice is "mother's milk" to Lottie—referring to the fact that after being weaned from the bottle (at thirteen months) Lottie practically stopped drinking milk, substituting orange juice and other fruit juices for her main liquid.

HUMOR, LAUGHTER, AND TEARS

The interplay between laughing and crying, shifting in significance through the first school period—against the background of Lottie's changing affective states—illuminates from another perspective Lottie's struggle to reduce the stress of her school experiences. The attempts at humor and the determined resistance to crying, already noted in other contexts, express Lottie's wide-ranging level of maturity, some latent wishes, and her poignant denial defense.

For the first three weeks of school, Lottie tries to laugh it off. But her jokes are overdone and her laughter has a hollow ring. It has been mentioned that, when Lottie falls off her chair at juice-time in the second session, she laughs uproariously and transforms it into a big joke by repeating it deliberately three times. The long-ago mastered art of chair-balance becomes a source of humor and a chance to act like a baby within the frame of the jest. Perhaps it also expresses her wish not to be at school: a baby doesn't go to school; 'on the chair, off the chair' may be enacting 'I'm here, I'm away from here'. It is later the same morning that she misnames her teacher. The laughing correction ("Not Miss Peters!") in effect recognizes and snatches back the meaning from her slip: 'I don't really wish that Miss Wilkins were Miss Peters, which would make me merely a school visitor (or, perhaps, Dorrie).' In 3, when Lottie laughs so intensely after her mother leaves her at school for the first time, calling out her family's names over and over at her locker—here, laughter apparently substitutes directly for tears: 'I want to cry so hard that I laugh.'

Mrs Baker describes Lottie entering school on the fifth morning as though she were "in a high drunk". This 'manic' mood is carried through in her juice-time rendition of the 'dry up' song —sung repeatedly, laughing "almost hysterically". This is a 'Dorrie' kind of song, probably learned by Lottie from her sister. It expresses defiance, in quasi-acceptable fashion (since it is in song form and employs a weakened synonym), by means of the invective forbidden to children against adults—'shut up'. In the context, Lottie may also be saying: 'Eat, drink, and be merry— for tomorrow we die, or rather, our mothers will leave us.' Not only is Dorrie, she says, but "Lottie's at kindergarten, too", contradicting her teacher. And on this day of reversal, it is she, Lottie, who tells her mother to leave. Thus, Lottie denies her reluctance to come to school (entering "in a high drunk"); denies her age and perhaps her identity (insisting on wearing a skirt like Dorrie's instead of overalls, and on being in kinder-garten rather than nursery school); denies her dependence on adults and compliance (the 'shut up' song); and, finally, denies her separation anxiety (ordering her mother to go). The mood of wild gaiety persists on the trip home with Lottie and Jeanie (of the fours) "whooping it up" in the car, laughing and jumping.

That this is denial through elation, rather than the start of a happy acceptance of school, is indicated by the exaggerated and transient nature of the hilarity and of the behavior which accompanies it.

Gaiety characterizes Lottie's arrival for the seventh session, belied only by Crying, the doll she carries with her. She reacts again with tense laughter ("not a fun laugh, almost hysterical, nervous") when a boy cries at his mother's leaving. Touched, perhaps too painfully, by his predicament, she laughs, instead of crying with him. When the mother returns with his small sister, Kaye, Lottie is delighted with this one-year-old. Lottie swings with her, talks about her "big Kaye" at home and cracks a joke at her own mother's expense:

LOTTIE   Is Kaye at nursery school?
MRS BAKER   No. She's in school at home.
LOTTIE   No, I mean *little* Kaye (*laughing triumphantly*).

Possibly reassured by the prompt return of the crying boy's mother, Lottie engages in a well-framed, more temperate form of humor. She mocks herself as well as her mother, incorporating two of her own current major concerns—exaggerating bigness versus littleness (the thirteen-year-old Kaye compared to the one-year-old) and also making fun of her wish to be at the older children's school by the ridiculous apposition of big Kaye's junior high school with little Kaye's visiting at nursery school. At the same time she traps her mother into an error, enjoying this more mature form of besting the adult.

The mood shifts in the next four sessions to a more serious one. Lottie emphatically refuses to let her mother go off for a while in 8. She enters quite happily, but she wants to leave when another girl screams for her mother, and she appears to be restless after this. The following session (9) is a quiet, observing day; Lottie is reluctant to go into school and seems tired there. Mrs Baker notes the lack of liveliness on the part of all the children in 10—"not in general a good day". On the eleventh morning Lottie ranges back and forth waiting for her painting turn. However, she can accept her mother's proposal to leave (the first separation of more

56

than a few minutes since the Lottie-directed departure of 5) and seems not to be affected by the crying around her, caused by all the mothers having left. For the next two mornings she continues to progress, managing separations of over an hour in a cheerful manner.

Here, during the second three weeks of school, Lottie apparently works out a different pattern of adjustment. No longer buoyed up by elation, she becomes at first serious and rather restless, then achieves, very briefly, manifest self-reliance and contentment in school. Probably this is based on her identification (more in action and mood now than in words) with Dorrie; she can 'be' a big five-year-old who lets her mother go, who paints pictures, and who shows no disturbance from the babyish crying of young children.

This too passes. For, as we have seen, with the revelation of the defense, "I am Dorrie" (14), comes the beginning of its relinquishment. Lottie enters school excited, tense, rather "high" (reminiscent of 5). Accepting her mother's leaving with minor, verbal objection, Lottie asks for her in mid-morning. On Mrs Baker's return, Lottie rushes to her mother, pulling at her, throwing toys, and smiling. In this first regressive, direct provocation of her mother at school, Lottie may be trying to minimize with her smiles the seriousness of her intent ('I don't really mean it, I'm just being silly').

At school during the next three mornings Lottie expresses more and more overtly her objection to being separated from her mother. Although she accepts her mother's going in 15, she clings to Mrs Baker on her return. When her mother tells Lottie that she plans to go shopping in the next session, Lottie objects strenuously: "I want you to stay, Mommy. Don't go." It is on this day that Lottie cries for her mother in school for the first time, after her mother has been gone for some time. Again in 17 she does not want Mrs Baker to leave and cries for her later ("real tears"). Finally, now the momentous eighteenth session: having attempted to defend herself with pseudo-elation and then with sister identification, Lottie faces separation as herself, a two-year-

57

old; she cries for her mother at the moment of separation, bursting into tears: "Don't go, Mommy." Moreover, Mrs Baker's reappearance after this separation is the occasion for Lottie's acceptance speech ("This is not Dorrie's school. This is Lottie's school").

Now that it is *her* school, Lottie cries next time again. Mrs Baker, waiting in the hall, hears her screaming. It lasts for about fifteen minutes, harder than she ever cries at home; it is more angry than sad, Mrs Baker reports, and devastating to hear. Mrs Baker wants to go right in, but Mrs Zerber, whom she has signalled through the door-window, asks her to wait a little while longer so that Miss Wilkins can handle it to the end. Very soon thereafter, Mrs Baker re-enters. Lottie is most happy to see her. She stays close, refusing to talk about where her mother was, and her play is turbulent and random; she goes from one thing to another, throwing toys (as in 14). She talks a great deal about Dorrie. Once, when Mrs Baker suggests she play with blocks, Lottie answers: "Dorrie? Where's Dorrie?" Mrs Baker repeats what she said. Lottie laughs: "Oh, I thought you said 'Dorrie'."

School is a serious place for Lottie the last three mornings before the vacation. In the car each day she must make sure her mother is staying with her: "Don't go bye-bye." She must keep close track of her mother in school. She expresses her feelings against her mother and school, clambering over Mrs Baker, building a tower of heavy blocks, only to send them crashing down in all directions.

VI

Winter

"You don't go away in nursery school.
You stay with me."

In the winter period (8 January to 14 March 1957) Lottie attended
sixteen of the twenty sessions of nursery school (23 through 38).
She missed three mornings in January and one in February.

During this middle third of the school year we shall see a new,
reworked version of autumn's separation story. The sequence
can be summarized briefly as reluctance and hesitation, holding
on to mother, denial of parting, return to crying, persistence of
crying, and, finally, acceptance of school with token tears.
However, the outstanding features of the period are the absence
of the exaggerated defenses of the fall and the far-reaching
developmental changes within Lottie, related to her discovery of
sex differences.

In this chapter the records of the first winter session of school
(23), and the home material of the day preceding and the day
following, are presented and discussed first. The themes which
emerge, with some additions, are then followed chronologically
in each successive month.

SCHOOL REOPENS

*7 January 1957. Record of the day before resumption of nursery
school*

Mr Baker told Lottie that he could take her to nursery school
the next day; she was delighted. A little while after, she said

59

to her mother: "You don't go away in nursery school. You stay with me." Mrs Baker reminded her that she had agreed to go with her daddy. Lottie: "You stay with me at nursery school." Mrs Baker said that they would decide the next day.

Later in the morning Mrs Baker was dashing up and down the stairs (very like the way she does on the mornings when she is getting ready to go to nursery school). Lottie said: "We're going to nursery school?" Mrs Baker said: "Not until tomorrow." Lottie: "Ohh."

In the afternoon Lottie, Dorrie, and Caron were dressing to go outdoors. Mrs Baker wanted Lottie to wear a sweater under her snowsuit. Lottie did not want to: "Is Dorrie wearing one?" When told yes, she wanted to know which one, went over to see, then agreed to put on a white one like Dorrie's. Outdoors, playing in the snow, Lottie had many troubles: she couldn't eat her raisins with her mittens on; she fell down; she hit herself in the eye. Each time Dorrie, with her arm around Lottie, as a comrade helps a wounded soldier, brought her to the back door for help.

Mrs Baker remarked that, in contrast to Lottie's humor about so many things, she is deadly serious in her imitation of Dorrie; always observing what Dorrie is wearing, eating, doing; waiting for Dorrie's pronouncements before making her own; changing her tune, if Dorrie does. The family have to hold themselves back from laughing at Lottie, sometimes it is so funny (but not to Lottie).

Mrs Baker went upstairs to take Heidi's temperature; Lottie went up saying: "Take it in the fanny. Take it in the fanny—then I can see Heidi's fanny!" Mrs Baker said she was taking it by mouth. When Heidi had the thermometer in her mouth, Lottie said, "It's in her fanny!"

Lottie loves to take baths with Dorrie. She asks her mother: "Can I have a bath with Dorrie?" If Mrs Baker says no, she asks: "Can I have a bath?" If the answer is no: "Can Heidi have a bath?" Once it was suggested, in fun, that she have a bath with Heidi. She thought that was terribly funny: "Heidi is too big!" When Lottie is asked how old she is, she answers "five" (Dorrie's age).

8 January 1957. Record of nursery-school session 23

Mrs Baker told Lottie the night before that she was to wear overalls to school and Mrs Baker laid them out for her. Lottie: "Is Dorrie going to wear a dress?" Mother: "Yes, but in your school you wear overalls."

In the morning Lottie did not get dressed with her sisters (as she often does). Mrs Baker questioned her about it. Lottie asked when Mrs Baker was getting dressed—"after breakfast" was the reply. Lottie said that she would wait too. There was more comment about Dorrie wearing a dress.

On the way to school, when Mrs Baker asked whom she would see there, Lottie said she was going to see Miss Wilkins and the two Alices. Lottie came in happily and eagerly (no hiding behind Mother's coat), even helped a little bit taking off her clothes at the locker. Then she paused—"I take your hand"—and went in with Mrs Baker to the big room. June's father was sitting in the one big chair. Lottie asked, "Where is June's Mommy?" Mrs Baker explained that June's father had brought her today. Miss Wilkins suggested that Lottie go with her to get a chair for Mommy. When they brought it back, Lottie wanted to sit on her mother's lap. Mrs Baker said no, she was going to read—Lottie could sit next to her and play. Lottie did not persist (as she had before the Christmas vacation) but sat next to Mrs Baker in the rocking-chair. Miss Wilkins invited her to join the play nearby with peg-boards. After a few minutes she went over and played. But when June took over the rocking-chair Lottie came back and demanded it. Miss Wilkins said there was another rocking-chair in the other room and Lottie went off with her to get it. Both June and Lottie rocked for a while until Lottie announced that she wanted to paint.

Miss Wilkins started to put an apron on her. Lottie refused. Miss Wilkins said: "Oh yes, you're the no-apron girl." Lottie painted, absorbed—using the four colors now given —a swirling, curving line picture with colors that came out unusually mixed together. She got a small amount of paint on her overalls and made a big point of it. While she was painting, some children started asking for juice and crackers. Miss Wilkins said that they would wait until a little later, until ten that morning. Lottie asked Mrs Baker to take her to the bathroom, where she again made her usual statement, "I don't fall in!" (Mrs Baker is always surprised that she still needs to comment about these especially small, easy toilets, when she can manage so well—usually now without comment—on the full-size toilet at home.)

Miss Wilkins read the book *Goodnight Moon* to a group of children including Lottie. Lottie listened with rapt attention, but (Mrs Baker felt) as if it were a completely new story to her (rather than an old favorite, known by heart and 'read' at home by Lottie to Mrs Baker, instead of vice versa). Miss Wilkins said it was juice- and cracker-time and Lottie was one of the first to bring her chair to the table (she did not involve Mrs Baker as she had in the past). Miss Wilkins gave out a whole double graham cracker (a special treat) to each child. Lottie broke hers and asked for another "whole one". Miss Wilkins said no, first finish that one. Lottie accepted this. They all had apple juice (the group were drinking and eating, Mrs Baker reported, as if they had had no nourishment for days). Lottie asked for some more "orange juice". Miss Wilkins said: "You're teasing! Does Dorrie tease a lot?" Lottie laughed and said yes.

After juice, the phonograph was brought out and most of the children brought up chairs to listen, but Lottie sat in the rocking-chair next to Mrs Baker. When she heard a Charity Bailey song, 'In the Kitchen', she said to June's father that she had that record at home. Mrs Baker (surprised that Lottie could recognize Charity Bailey) explained to Lottie that she had another Charity Bailey record at home, but not this one. Lottie then repeated this to June's father. Another record was put on and most of the group got up to dance—jumping, running, pushing, bumping. Lottie joined in this and stopped by to tell Mrs Baker, "I like Larry!" Then she made a dash for him which he fended off, but in a friendly manner. June's father was bouncing June on his knee to the music and Lottie asked to go on too. Then little Alice came and he had three girls going "horsey".

When the hamsters were brought down from the piano, Miss Wilkins invited Lottie to play with them. She said: "I sit on your lap"—and from that vantage point she played with them, quite roughly, remarking how they tickled her. When Miss Wilkins had to leave the room for a few minutes, the assistant teacher took over and Lottie stayed, in the same chair. There was another trip later that Lottie went on. Each time, when she returned from these excursions out of the room, she ran happily over to her mother. (Mrs Baker feels that Lottie gets special pleasure out of these trips, not only for themselves, but also from leaving her mother in the room and finding her again on her return—just as Mrs Baker has left Lottie in order to make telephone calls and go shopping.)

Lottie went again to the bathroom, this time by herself. When she came out she claimed that her pants were wet and she needed to change. Miss Wilkins couldn't feel any wetness, but Lottie insisted on changing. When Miss Wilkins brought out a pair of school pants, Lottie exclaimed: "They're yellow!" There was a just noticeable washed-out, faint print of yellow flowers on the pants.

Lottie played with little Alice, stringing beads—both talking and laughing animatedly. Lottie said: "A green one. Alice Wollstein has a green one!" Then she picked up the rhyme, something like: "Alice Wollstein has a green! Alice Wollstein has a green!" They started to scream, each time looking at Miss Wilkins for a response. So much so that Miss Wilkins finally said: "Do you want me to ask you to stop?

63

But it's all right if you want to." After they had completed their strings, they flung them down. Then the beads were thrown out of the box, all around. Mrs Baker asked them to pick them up. Miss Wilkins seconded her, suggesting a pick-up time. Lottie and Alice both helped cheerfully. (Mrs Baker does not think it is good for Lottie to engage in wild, wanton behavior with no bounds. She was pleased that Miss Wilkins backed her on the picking-up suggestion.)

While Lottie was playing, a father came in and talked quietly with Miss Wilkins nearby about his son's morning. Miss Wilkins remarked that he had enjoyed playing with the hamsters. Whereupon the father said that he liked to play with them too and had been in yesterday with a little girl. At this point Lottie interrupted, joining the conversation: "Did you play with the hamsters?"—"The little girl goes to nursery school?" Before anyone knew what was happening, the father was carrying on a conversation with Lottie rather than with Miss Wilkins. Miss Wilkins explained to Lottie that sometimes children who go to other schools visit nursery school.

While she was getting ready to go home, Mrs Baker asked Lottie if she wanted to take her painting. She did and Mrs Baker started to look around for it. There were a great many paintings up on the walls. Lottie quickly pointed out her own across the room. Lottie hugged Miss Wilkins goodbye and threw a kiss to Mrs Zerber. On the way out Lottie remarked that the water in the sink was running. Sure enough, there was a very slight trickle. She dashed off to Jean's room to pick her up.

In the afternoon (8 January 1957), Lottie told me about school: "I didn't cry. I got paint on my overalls."

Mrs Baker described some of Lottie's current concerns. She feels that Lottie is very "compulsive". She wonders if it is just a stage. At school Lottie is bothered by a paint spot on her overalls, even though she refuses to wear an apron, and she notices the water dripping far off in the sink. At home she is particularly meticulous and insistent about clothes and going to bed. Not only must Lottie's undershirt be tucked into her pants just so (which Mrs Baker instituted) but each seam of clothing must be lined up perfectly. At bedtime the bed must be absolutely clear, the covers tucked in tight. She must work her way under the tucked covers, then they must be adjusted again. A song must be sung, the rhyme said: "Good night. Sleep tight. Don't let the bedbugs bite." Part of the latest bedtime routine involves a set questioning of her mother:

LOTTIE   You get into your pajamas and come into my bed with me. Why not?

MOTHER   I can't, because I have work to do.

LOTTIE   No. You can't because you sleep with Daddy in your own bed. Say it.

MOTHER   I sleep in my own bed with Daddy.

Before bed, she always runs to the mirror in Heidi's room —first with her slip on, and then nude—to parade and look at herself.

9 January 1957

At dinner Mr Baker was talking with the girls (giving Lottie a chance to talk too) but Lottie got noisier and noisier. Her father told her to quiet down—with no effect. Then he told her angrily and loudly to stop at once. She cried very hard, reaching out to Mrs Baker: "Mommy, Mommy." When she didn't stop, her mother told her to go into the living room and to come back when she had calmed down. She went in, cried for several minutes, then returned. When her father came to her later to clear things up, she turned from him and would not accept a reconciliation. On the stairs, going up with her mother to bed, she said proudly: "I didn't say goodnight to Daddy." Mrs Baker: "That was wrong of you." (Mrs Baker wondered later, how can one talk that way to a two-year-old? Yet Lottie elicits this.)

In these records of the time of the reopening of school in January, almost all of the major themes of the winter period can be discerned.

Lottie, now two years and seven months, has moved from a primary relationship at home with her mother to a triangular one involving her father. She has become acutely aware of him and manifestly ambivalent in her feelings.

She seems delighted when Mr Baker says that he can take her to school the first morning, but is adamant that her mother must be there: "You don't go away in nursery school. You stay with me." It is Mrs Baker who takes Lottie to school. There, Lottie is drawn to two visiting fathers; she manages to involve herself with both during the morning. When she finds June's father in the room, she immediately asks where June's mother is. Later, Lottie converses with him about a record and finally, at her own request, joins June in bouncing on his knee to the music. When another father comes in to talk with Miss Wilkins, Lottie breaks in, redirecting the talk about hamsters and a little girl to a conversation between herself and the father.

Only the attraction component of her attitude to fathers emerges at school (even when finally, at the eleventh winter session, Lottie's own father brings her); but at home the battle lines are drawn as Lottie struggles with her difficult transitional relationship to her father. Lottie's current bedtime ritual reveals most clearly her conception of her father as the successful rival for her mother's love. It is so characteristic of Lottie that she must state both the wish (to have her mother come to bed with her) and the wish-denying reality (mother sleeps with father in their bed). She will not accept her mother's refusal on the less painful, less direct grounds of "work to do". But she, Lottie, puts the words of truth in her mother's mouth and issues the order: "Say it." Only thus, perhaps, can she accept the sad reality, by dominating and controlling it through words that she

66

says herself and forces her mother to repeat. Lottie, at this time, does sometimes clash directly with her father. At dinner on the day following 23 she ignores his requests to quiet down, provokes him to be sharp with her, then bursts into crying and turns to her mother. It is Mrs Baker who sends her out of the room to calm down. But Lottie will not accept a reconciliation with her father afterwards. She goes off to bed, still defiant, proudly announcing to her mother that she has not said goodnight to him.

Lottie is far from ready to go to school and stay without her mother this first morning of the winter period. Nevertheless, a strikingly different picture is presented from that of the last day at school before the vacation. During that session (22) she spent half the morning on her mother's lap and then violently threw the chairs down when Mrs Baker asked her to get off, suggesting that Lottie sit on a nearby chair if she needed to be close. In 23, to be sure, she demands her mother's presence at school, takes her hand on entering the big room, and at first wants to sit on her lap. But after a few minutes of sitting in a chair next to Mrs Baker, Lottie ranges far and wide, participating in activities and relating to children and adults in a free, lively manner far beyond anything reported during the fall. Lottie's behavior pattern this first day of school is in the form of a rondo: ABACADA. . . . 'Stay-close-to-mother' is the major theme, stated on entering school ("I take your hand"). She goes to get a chair for her mother and sits next to her. Only then can she play another tune, accepting Miss Wilkins's invitation to use the peg-board. Noticing that June has taken over 'her' chair, Lottie returns to rocking next to her mother. Reassured, she decides to paint. Then back she goes to Mother, this time with a request to be taken to the bathroom. She can leave again to hear a book and to partake of juice and crackers, returning afterwards to her chair. Then she ventures out to join in the dancing. Thus it goes the entire morning, being with Mother, going off, back to Mother —away and return.

This day seems to be a statement of Lottie's potential for nursery school, a potential not to be fully realized independently (that is, without the presence of her mother) until a new three-month variation of the separation drama has been enacted.

New areas have opened up for Lottie. A favorite home book, read to her by her mother a hundred times, can now be listened to and reacted to at school. A favorite home singer is recognized when played on records at school. At last Lottie's separated images of home and school worlds are becoming merged into one extended world. She not only reacts freely with adults, but she is relating to other children in a manner rarely seen in her at school before. While dancing, she stops by to tell her mother that she likes Larry and then makes a friendly-aggressive dash for him. Later in the morning there is a joint play sequence with another girl: stringing beads, a Lottie-invented name-color rhyme (using the *other* child's name), screaming, throwing of strings and beads, and, finally, picking up. This authority-baiting, bounds-testing behavior involves several unique characteristics. It is co-peer: Lottie joins together with another child, rather than standing alone. It is directed against the teacher: previously her mother has been the main target. It is light and gay in tone, in contrast to the serious, angry, or over-silly quality of earlier wild play. It is terminated by setting to rights: willing participation in cleaning up. It should be noted that, in addition to new achievements, the gains of the fall period have not been lost. Her teacher is a familiar, trusted adult. Lottie accepts Miss Wilkins's invitations to join in various activities and goes on her lap to play with the hamsters. She can even remain with the assistant teacher when Miss Wilkins leaves. Lottie requests painting—this most enjoyed activity of the fall period. She has maintained (after the first time) her bathroom and juice-time independence. She goes off happily on several small trips away from the room.

The rapid development in the fall of Lottie's relationship to her sister Dorrie into a strong identification was traced out in Chapter V. It was shown how, in the course of working out her adjustment to school, Lottie apparently protected herself for a time against the full impact of separation from her mother by utilizing this identification as a defense. Lottie's behavior in school, it will be recalled, regressed markedly after her dramatic announcement in the autumn period relinquishing this identification defense. Now, at the start of winter, Lottie is observing, comparing herself with, and imitating Dorrie as doggedly as ever in the home. She says she is five when asked her age. At times she seems hardly to make a move without consulting her perception of Dorrie. However, in school she is free of the sister identification at the manifest level. She no longer employs this defense there, nor does she return to it again in any obvious, pervasive form during the school year. Whether or not the stress of beginning school was a major or minor factor in the genesis of the sister identification, it is clear that Lottie actively carried it over from home into the school situation for only a relatively short period. Furthermore, it is apparent that this identification with her sister continues to flourish at home well after it has been given up at school.

Two other themes emerge from the first days' records that reappear repeatedly throughout the winter period. One theme concerns Lottie's extremely meticulous and demanding behavior about clothing. What she is to wear, how it is to be worn, the necessity to change at the slightest spot or wetness—about all these aspects of clothing, she feels deeply and reacts strongly. Her compulsiveness, as Mrs Baker terms it, extends further to the arrangement of the bed-clothes and the nightly bedtime ritual. The final theme from these records involves Lottie's manifest preoccupation with bodily functions and sex differences. When her mother is about to take Heidi's temperature, Lottie urges: "Take it in the fanny—then I can see Heidi's fanny!" Heidi has the thermometer in her mouth, but Lottie persists, "It's in her fanny!" At bedtime Lottie must look at herself nude in the mirror and must exchange the ritual words with her mother on the subject of Mother sleeping with Father and not with Lottie.

JANUARY

In January Lottie attended five sessions of nursery school (23 through 27); she missed three mornings because of bad driving conditions. These absences were distributed so that during the first, second, and fourth weeks Lottie attended school only once, instead of twice, a week.

From Lottie's separation behavior this first month of the winter period, one could almost believe that she was just now beginning school. The crucial events of the fall period—the attempts to cope with school and mother separation by a manic mood and identification with the sister, the eventual giving up of these defenses with the breakthrough of feelings of helplessness and rage in crying and regressive behavior forcing the mother to stay—all these experiences seem almost to have been wiped away. Lottie, these early winter mornings of school, appears to start anew—slowly, begrudgingly, but without much expression of affect, accepting her mother's leaving her at school for increasing periods.

Lottie turns down her father's invitation to take her to school for the second session (24). She shows some independence on entering: she helps to take off her clothes and plays at her locker while her mother goes into the main room to sit down. Mrs Baker leaves briefly twice to telephone. The first time, Lottie wants to go with her, and sits in her mother's chair when she leaves. However, she is painting when Mrs Baker returns. The second time, Lottie asks, "Did you bring me a prize?" when her mother comes back.

Lottie enters in good spirits on the following morning, gaily tells Miss Wilkins that she is wearing Caron's jumper. She goes frequently to her mother, who is reading, but she also participates in many activities and accepts Mrs Baker's absence of a few minutes.

On the way to the fourth winter session of school (26) Mrs Baker mentions going off to buy candles for Dorrie's birthday. Lottie responds emphatically: "Mommy come to school with me!" But she is less hesitant and clinging coming into the locker room. She helps to take off her clothes and goes into the main room without waiting for her mother. While Mrs Baker sits reading, Lottie comes over to her frequently, yet she shows no need to stay at her side. In the middle of the morning Lottie herself tells her mother to go get the candles. (This recalls the fifth session in the fall when Lottie first told Mrs Baker to leave school.) After one hour Mrs Baker returns and is met happily by Lottie.

On the last day of January (27) Lottie seems to accept her mother's remark, on the way to school, that she will go shopping later. But there is less bounce on entering and Lottie's participation in school activities is half-hearted. When Mrs Baker says that she is leaving, Lottie does not look at her mother or respond. Mrs Baker goes to get her coat and comes back to say goodbye again; this time Lottie answers: "Bring me a prize." At the end of the morning Mrs Baker returns. Lottie's greeting is: "I didn't cry."

"How was school today?", I ask that afternoon. "I didn't cry" is the first response. Only then does Lottie go on to mention clay and painting. Lottie wants and needs to cry when her mother leaves her at school, but this she does not permit herself. Rather than cry, she first attempts to deny her mother's departure by not responding to the farewell, and then, her denial not accepted, she restructures the separation as a shopping trip to buy a present for herself.

Thus, at the end of three and a half weeks and five school sessions, Lottie has attained about the same degree of acceptance of separation from her mother as she seemed to have achieved after two months and fourteen school sessions in the fall. This new version of working-through-separation is considerably pared down and tightened in its structure; the earlier themes of over-elation and sister identification are eliminated. However, Lottie still has not reached a comfortable, easy acceptance of her mother's leaving her in school. There remains an artificial and defensive quality to her behavior.

If mother separation must be worked through all over again, this is not true of Lottie's general acceptance of school. As the record of the first winter school day revealed, teacher, children, and activities are familiar and safe. Lottie's participation has expanded rather than contracted after the three weeks' vacation from school.

The hamsters continue to be a target for furious delight. During 24, Lottie is with Miss Wilkins at the hamsters' glass cage:

LOTTIE	They're looking at me! They're laughing at me! They're biting me! Not really. (*Lottie grabs both hamsters. Miss Wilkins holds one of her hands.*) Let go of my hand!
MISS WILKINS	I can't. Better put one back.
LOTTIE	I'll hold it still! (*Lottie puts one back; then she grabs two again.*)
	(*At the end of the morning Miss Wilkins gives Lottie a hug.*)
MISS WILKINS	Did you have as good a morning as I did?
	(*Lottie smiles.*)

In 26 Lottie finds a jump-rope. Holding it a few inches off the ground, she jumps over it. Larry comes and demands the rope, but Lottie refuses to give it to him. Miss Wilkins explains that it is Larry's own rope from home and he will keep it in his locker. Lottie gives up the rope with reluctance and goes quickly over to her mother. Later, during music, she plays especially with Larry in a teasing way.

These January mornings in school are active ones for Lottie. In addition to joining in music and playing with the hamsters, she paints during every session, uses beads, puzzles, blocks, and clay, and is absorbed in the doll corner putting the dolls to bed. One painting, from 26, consists of a few red brushstrokes and groups of five lines in different colors: the effect is achieved by dipping the fingers of both hands in the paints and drawing the fingertips across the paper to make thin parallel lines. Mrs Baker notices, in January and February, that Lottie shows great interest when boys come out of the lavatory, with diapers and overalls down, to be helped. She often calls out, "See his fanny!"

In the January home records, certain incidents reveal some of the underlying trends in Lottie's behavior. When her sisters return to public school, the week before nursery school reopens, Lottie announces:

"I go to nurserygarten. Dorrie goes to kindergarten. Soon I go to kindergarten and first grade in public school."

Each word is pronounced carefully and deliberately as if it were a lesson learned by rote. It is all apparently accepted and clear to her now. Only the neologism, which serves to minimize the difference between her school and Dorrie's, and the artificial mode of speech, reveal remnants of her original insistence that she too was going to kindergarten.

Though Lottie has begun to participate more freely at school in activities long enjoyed at home, home is still the primary source for new skills and mastery. She goes ice-skating for the first time, doing well on double-runner skates. She is fascinated by the phenomenon of the layer of ice over water. At the edge of the town pond, where she skates, a waterfall pours out below the frozen surface; she must go as close as possible to investigate. She jokes: "We go swimming?", and on her return home she drapes a hat over herself, laughing: "It's my bathing suit!"

A few days before school begins, Lottie comes to my house for her naptime. As she climbs into the large double bed, she says she is going to sleep with Caron's Daddy. She also invites me, Dorrie, and Caron to join her in bed. All of her clothes are taken off, except the slip:

I   Do you sleep in your slip?
LOTTIE Mommy lets me!
I   O.K.
LOTTIE Not really (taking off the slip).

From Kaye has come down to all the girls the phrase "not really"; it is slipped in quickly after a statement of fact which is not true. Lottie enjoys doing what she knows is not permitted. But if she goes uncorrected, then she herself must confess or undo the forbidden act.

73

There are several home-separation experiences during this period. During the vacation the family goes to the city; Lottie and her sisters sleep overnight at their aunt's apartment while Mr and Mrs Baker stay elsewhere. Lottie asks for her mother at bedtime, speaks with her on the telephone then, and in the morning again; she is reported to have managed quite well. The weekend after school begins (23-24) Mr and Mrs Baker go away for three days, leaving Lottie and her sisters for two nights at my house.

11 January 1957. Record of Lottie's stay at my house with her sisters while her parents are away for the weekend

I was cutting a chocolate Santa Claus into three parts:

LOTTIE   He cries.

I   It's just a chocolate Santa Claus. It can't cry.

LOTTIE   She can cry—*pretend*.

Later, Caron and I were going through Caron's books making piles of them to lend to Lottie and Dorrie. Lottie sat in a small chair, quietly 'reading' each one in her pile: "Is this mine?" She was especially delighted with M. W. Brown's *Home for a Bunny*—"Oh, a bunny! Read it!" I read it to her several times during the two days. Lottie made many comments: "I don't like this one (the frog)—I like him (the groundhog). Oh, the bunny—I love him. (Then the white bunny) I love him and him (both white and brown)." She curves her arms to the page as if to hug both rabbits. After reading the book at naptime, she quoted it—"Can I come in?"—just before slipping under the tightly tucked covers for her nap.

At lunch Lottie started singing 'Polly put the kettle on'. Pretty soon, with Caron and Dorrie joining in, they substituted "penis", "vulva", and "BM"—Lottie being a leader as much as a follower in this. When I stopped the big girls by saying it wasn't polite lunch-table singing, they shifted to other songs. But Lottie continued with several more 'verses'.

74

At naptime Lottie asked me: "Do you have a vulva?"

The girls were calling themselves by their middle names. Caron was "Margo", Dorrie "Sally", Lottie "Ann". But Lottie insisted that *she* was Sally and Dorrie was Ann.

The three Degas nude-bather drawings in the bathroom elicited much comment from Lottie. She first noticed the one of a woman stepping into the tub: "See her fanny! BMs coming out!" (I explained that it was a shadow, not BM.) Lottie persisted: "BM coming out! Where's her leg?" (I showed her that one leg was hidden in the bathtub.) Then there were remarks about the other two pictures of women drying themselves after the bath.

Caron, Dorrie, and Lottie played out in the snow and went for a hike in the woods in the afternoon with Heidi and Kaye. Before supper, Lottie, Dorrie, and Caron had a joint bath with much gaiety and splashing and helping each other. Lottie made sure her towels were hanging neatly and exactly, next to Dorrie's.

Mr and Mrs Baker telephoned just after supper and spoke to the three girls. Lottie went to bed cheerfully and fell asleep promptly. But at 2 a.m. she woke up and there followed a period of two and a half hours in which she was awake—sometimes crying, sometimes laughing and talking, sometimes in bed, sometimes wandering around, asking to have her barrette put back in, and so forth. (She had had a wakeful period at this part of the night a few times at home in the fall, but not for several months.) At one point Caron and Lottie had a conversation in which Caron suggested that Lottie rest quietly in bed, think about tomorrow, and soon she would fall asleep. Lottie replied that she couldn't because her mommy was away. I went in many times, comforting and settling, finally threatening that I would have to move Lottie out of the girls' room. When nothing worked, and both Caron and Dorrie were wide awake, I moved Lottie and her bed into my room. Lottie was very quiet and soon asleep. She woke about 7.30 a.m. for the day. On Saturday Lottie got up in the middle of her naptime and came out all dressed. I very firmly put her back to bed, whereupon she slept for an hour and a half. She woke up irritable, but after a while (she went ice-skating with me and all the girls) became quite gay. She was very charming and hungry at dinner. She accepted going to bed in my room and slept through the night—although she whimpered some in her sleep. Once, when it sounded as if Lottie were about to cry, I went to check her and found her asleep on the floor next to her low bed. She did not wake up when she was put back and tucked in.

Caron came in the back door in the afternoon and Lottie said, laughing, with an artificially gay tone: "Oh, I thought it was Mommy coming in!" Lottie and I talked many times about where Mommy and Daddy were and when they were coming home. On Saturday Lottie even voiced some regret that this was to be the last night at my house (but, as Lottie would say, "not really"). When Mrs Baker came on Sunday, Lottie greeted her most happily. A little later, during a puppet show put on by Heidi, Dorrie, and Caron, Lottie was extremely disruptive and negative—insisting on taking part instead of watching. But then she recovered her good spirits and maintained them later at home.

This record of Lottie's behavior during a home separation from her parents reveals—more directly than her behavior at school—some of the fantasies that preoccupy her at this time. Her concern about body damage and sex differences, as well as her unflagging interest in the anal sphere, emerge in the incident of the cut-up chocolate Santa Claus who cries, the scatological song, and the comments about the nude drawings. She demonstrates her continuing home identification with her sister Dorrie in the game of middle names. The separation from her mother is difficult to bear, even cushioned as it is by the presence of her sisters in a familiar home. Lottie's mother is on her mind; she is awake several hours in the night saying that she cannot sleep because her mother is away; someone comes in the door and she thinks that it is her mother returning. When her mother does come back, Lottie's generally cheerful and cooperative behavior of the weekend temporarily deteriorates: she becomes negative and irritable—perhaps in retaliation against her mother for having left her.

In the following record of Dorrie's birthday party, near the end of the month (26-27), we can see that Lottie apparently feels herself to be more than a full participant; she behaves as if it were her own celebration. Not satisfied with the special presents for her, she keeps asking for more. She abstains only from hide-and-go-seek, staying near the mothers. The blindfold game she not only takes part in, but wins. Then, with high spirits, she stuffs herself with party fare and dominates the festivities at the table.

25 January 1957. Record of Dorrie's birthday party

At Dorrie's birthday party there were seven girls (five to six years of age), Heidi and Kaye as helpers, and Lottie. Lottie sat with the group on the floor while Dorrie opened the presents, saying: "Where are my presents? Is this mine?" She did get two little presents, but she kept asking for more. Throughout the games she kept asking her mother in the kitchen, *when* would they have the "party" (the food)? She ate a great deal of candy. While the girls dashed all over the house playing 'sardines', she stayed mostly in the living room (where the mothers were) hiding behind a big chair. When the time came for 'pin-the-tail-on-the-donkey', Lottie took her turn (she did not mind the blindfold) and her tail ended up the closest; she won. But before the game was over she had come into the kitchen, where final preparations were being made for the birthday supper, and started to help herself to potato chips. At the table she joined in the play, ate with great gusto (consuming large quantities of olives and potato chips and some hamburger), talking and blowing

77

into the telephone prizes and eating all the candy. Finally, at the end, she stood up in her chair yelling out: "Oh, they don't wear pants on the sunny side of France!"

FEBRUARY

Lottie attends seven of the eight sessions. Her one absence is caused by missing the bus. February is the crying month. It takes Lottie six sessions of the winter period (to 28) to bring herself to cry again in school. In the fall, it was not until the sixteenth morning of school that Lottie first cried. On both of these occasions the crying occurs, not at the moment of her mother's departure, but later, while Mrs Baker is away.

On the way to school for the twenty-eighth session Mrs Baker tells Lottie she will be going off with me. Lottie enters in high spirits and she goes right over to Miss Wilkins at the table. At juice-time Mrs Baker says that it is time for her to go. Lottie asks her to stay a few minutes longer. When her mother does leave, Lottie says goodbye from Miss Wilkins's lap. An hour and a half later, Lottie greets her mother from the top of the slide, all smiles: "Mommy! Mommy!" and then, "I cried." Miss Wilkins confirms that Lottie has cried; but, she says, it was not serious. Kent's father tells of Lottie being on his lap.

Before 29, Mrs Baker says that she will stay in the hall. When they arrive, Kent is crying; his father has just left. Miss Wilkins has to comfort him throughout the morning as he keeps starting up again. All the children seem quite affected; they are quiet when he cries and they talk about it when he stops. Miss Wilkins discusses it with the group: this is Kent's trouble; they will help him. Mrs Baker says that she is leaving. Lottie says "O.K." But Kent starts to cry again. Then Lottie says, "No. Don't go." Miss Wilkins comes and holds Lottie, saying that there is a lot of commotion and Mother should wait in the hall. Lottie says, "Kiss me." Then Mrs Baker leaves. After an hour, she returns. Lottie has cried a little bit and asked for her mother, Miss Wilkins reports, but she was readily comforted.

78

At the bus stop Mrs Baker and Lottie have a serious talk:

MRS BAKER School is for children to go to, not for grown-
ups to stay.
LOTTIE (*Interrupting*) But Wilkins is there!
MRS BAKER She is your teacher. She is there to take care of
you. (*Lottie gives a broad smile.*) As soon as children are used to school, parents don't stay any
more. Kent is having trouble getting used to it.
But you are used to it now. And next time
Daddy will take you and Mommy will come to
pick you up.
LOTTIE (*Smiling*) Daddy will take me!
MRS BAKER But Daddy can't stay. He will have to go right
to work.

Lottie apparently agrees to this plan. However, because of
changes in his work schedule, her father does not take her until
almost three weeks later. The following school morning Mrs
Baker and Lottie miss the bus. For days Lottie recounts this
experience, with as much regret (Mrs Baker says) for missing
the bus ride as for missing school.

On 30, Lottie enters school with "the usual hesitation".
Mrs Baker has errands to do and Miss Wilkins suggests that she
leave right away. Lottie cries very hard. Mrs Baker stays until
she calms down, then goes. She finds Lottie playing happily
on her return. It has taken eight sessions of the winter period
for Lottie to return to the direct expression of her feelings (which
had come after eighteen sessions of the fall)—to cry at the time
of separation.

Thus it seems that before Lottie can accept school separation
she must give up her defenses and suffer through the experience
directly. Although, as we have seen, she reached this point late
in the fall, Lottie's reaction was so strong that her mother stayed
at school with her for the subsequent four sessions. Then the
vacation intervened. This break in the continuity of school

attendance is followed by a change in Lottie's developing separation reaction. She does not continue to demand her mother's constant presence when school reopens as she did just before the vacation. Nor does she return to an entirely fresh start. But beginning, as it were, some steps beyond where she was at the opening of school, Lottie uses less extreme defenses in the winter period and requires less time to reach the point of allowing herself to feel the direct impact of separation.

During the next session, in which her older sister and a friend come to visit, Lottie slips back into using a denial defense. Heidi and Kaye come to school with Lottie and Mrs Baker on 31. Lottie is very gay and shows no hesitation entering. When her mother explains that she and the big girls can stay only a little while, Lottie says that she wants to go too. Heidi and Kaye leave after a few minutes, but Mrs Baker stays. Kent cries very hard when his mother goes. Miss Wilkins talks to Lottie about her mother's leaving and Kent's having a difficult time. When Mrs Baker is ready to go, Lottie ignores her; she will not look at her or speak. Finally she does say goodbye. On Mrs Baker's return, an hour later, Lottie bursts out: "You came back! You came back!"—as if, as Kaye remarks later, she did not expect her mother ever to return. There is no record for 32, when Dorrie and Caron come with Lottie to visit school.

Lottie's father takes her to school for the first time for the thirty-third session. Mrs Baker reports that she was very angry with Lottie for fighting with Heidi the night before, over undressing; she spanked her. That morning there is fighting again between them over clothes and the same piercing screams on Lottie's part. Still feeling angry, Mrs Baker tells Lottie the plan: her father will take her to school; he will *not* be able to stay; Mommy will pick her up. She was fully prepared, if Lottie were to object, to say, "All right then, no school." However, Lottie accepts the proposal with glee—to go with her father in his new car is a special treat. Later, she talks about Mommy going too; Mrs Baker makes it clear that *this* is the arrangement.

At school, Mr Baker walks down the hall past the room and

Lottie draws him back, laughing: "Here's my door!" Immediately upon entering, Mr Baker feels a change in Lottie. Suddenly she cannot do anything for herself. After sliding, she takes him, rather reluctantly, on a tour of the room: the hamsters, the fish, "Mommy's chair". He steps away from her and she dashes over and grabs his leg: "Don't go, Daddy. Don't go!" He explains that he is just going to talk with Miss Wilkins. Kent arrives, crying. Everything stops. They all look and listen. When his mother leaves, Kent cries again and he is given some candy. Finally, Mr Baker tells Lottie that he must go to his work (about twenty minutes after their arrival); she starts to cry. Miss Wilkins says that she has candy for her. A minute later Mr Baker looks through the door-window and sees Lottie smiling up at Miss Wilkins.

Lottie rushes over to her mother when she comes to call for her. She has had a good morning. But she does not want to stay while Mrs Baker picks up Jean; she goes right with her. On the way out Lottie and Miss Wilkins have a conversation:

MISS WILKINS   You had a *good* morning, Lottie.
LOTTIE   I cried.
MISS WILKINS   Yes, you cried. But then you felt all right.

At lunch, Lottie tells me about school: "I cried and I had candy —chocolate with chocolate sprinkles." It is noteworthy that Lottie reacts to her father's leaving her at school in the same way as to her mother's. The intricacies of her relationship to him at home, her ambivalence and rivalry, do not affect her pattern of reaction to separation in school. (Possibly, her mother's anger facilitated Lottie's initial acceptance of her father in the taking-to-school role.)

On the night before the thirty-fourth session Mrs Baker tells Lottie that she will take her to school and then go right off to art class. In the morning, as if she were continuing this conversation, Lottie suddenly says: "Don't go. Stay with me." Her mother repeats the plan. There is the usual slowdown on entering the schoolroom. Mrs Baker starts to leave immediately. Lottie sobs in Miss Wilkins's arms, reaching out for her mother: "Don't go.

Don't go. I want to go with you to your school." Mrs Baker feels terrible; she does not want to leave Lottie in this state and yet she thinks it is better not to prolong the parting. She does go right out of the room. Lottie's crying lasts about three minutes.

On Mrs Baker's return at the end of the morning, Lottie is absorbed in building with small blocks at a table. She throws herself into her mother's arms. However, this time, she returns immediately to her building. She shows Mrs Baker the school socks she is wearing because she wet herself. Miss Wilkins says Lottie had a fine morning, finger-painting and painting. She wet herself because she was too busy and absorbed to get to the bathroom on time. Mrs Baker remarks that Lottie does not have trouble in this area. She was not disturbed, Miss Wilkins adds, rather she seemed to enjoy it and was delighted to have school clothes put on.

Perhaps this first and only urinary lapse that Lottie 'permits herself' at school is not only a faint echo of the regressive behavior of the late fall against her mother, but signifies also the narrowing of the gap between school and home. (Lottie's non-accidental form of wetting at home is described below.) For Lottie, this is 'letting herself go' at school. She apparently feels free to 'test' Miss Wilkins. It seems to be carefree. The wetting may also be related to her feelings about the boys she observes so closely who wet themselves at school. It will be recalled that Lottie had just three urinary accidents at home before the vacation. There was also, during autumn, the pattern of slight, toidy-chair wetting of pants that were not pulled down far enough. Lottie has continued in the winter to wet herself at home, not through loss of control, but in a new, special manner. By deliberately leaning back on her small toidy-chair, Lottie manages to spray out the urine onto her pants, which she now carefully pushes way down to the floor, presumably to avoid wetness. Immediately, she must change into dry clothes. She is doing and undoing. With great control, she achieves the results of loss of control. In a feminine fashion, she imitates the masculine role. Then all must be set to rights; cleanliness and dryness are quickly reinstated.

82

This wetting-drying behavior is characteristic during the entire winter at home, although there are most references to it in February. It appears to be related to several other behaviors of the same period. In addition to pants being wet by sprayed urine, there are always socks soaked in puddles on the floor from the sink in Heidi's room. Then, besides the constant necessary renewal of pants and socks, Lottie will change her outer outfit several times a day, if permitted, adorning herself in her favorite dresses. She continues to object to the overalls which her mother insists that she wear for school and persists in her refusal of a school apron for painting. By the end of the month, she engages in fierce fights with Heidi almost every morning over the clothes laid out for her by her mother. Moreover, she is often discontented and complaining throughout the day at home about what she is wearing. "I need privacy!" is the frequent cry as Lottie goes off by herself to undress.

This restless dissatisfaction with body covering may express Lottie's inner turmoil over the recent discovery of her own sex identity. For this is a time of increasing sex talk: there is free use of the terms penis and vulva, often Dorrie-instigated, and many questions are asked about sexual matters. At the beginning of the month Lottie turns to her father at the table saying: "I don't like you because you have a penis." Her mother tells Lottie to say goodnight to her father, some days later. Lottie responds: "No. I won't say goodnight because you have a penis." About mid-February Lottie learns that her father sleeps without pajamas. She immediately wants to do the same. She comments on the fact that he does wear pajamas at breakfast and she frequently watches him shave in shorts. One night, at dinner, Dorrie whispers something to Lottie who then calls out: "Pour milk on Daddy's penis!"

The following record of one of Lottie's 'bad' days (32-33) illustrates the way in which Lottie's discontent with herself and her provocation of others are centered in the sphere of clothing. Just as she expressed in her fall behavior: 'I could manage nursery school and separation from Mother if I were Dorrie', she seems

83

to say now: 'If I could be (dressed like) Dorrie, then I could be content as a girl.' The dissatisfaction and baiting extend also into the food area. Lottie prolongs the provocation until, finally, she is spanked by her mother. Only after this unusually severe punishment does Lottie settle down contentedly.

24 February 1957. Record of one of Lottie's bad days

In the afternoon Lottie, Dorrie, and Heidi came with Mrs Baker to my house. While Lottie and Dorrie were undress-ing, Lottie complained that she didn't have on a "kitty-cat" dress like Dorrie's (this had been talked about in the morning too). Mrs Baker told her again that she had on a fine jumper and that there was no kitty-cat dress in her size. (Caron has the same dress as Dorrie, but she wasn't wearing it.) Dorrie took off her dress to put on a paper (cleaner's bag) mouse outfit; Caron was wearing a paper Cinderella dress. Lottie fussed. She insisted on taking off her jumper and then she wanted her blouse off. Mrs Baker refused. Lottie cried a bit and complained, but she never did put on the other Cin-derella dress that was available for her. She asked for refresh-ments and she was given orange juice, toast, and a lollipop. She claimed that the toast was not buttered sufficiently. She was very discontented. Finally the three girls went out-doors and played for some time with only a few mishaps. Lottie insisted on having bare legs like Dorrie, although Mrs Baker wanted her to wear slacks (Caron wore snow pants). When Lottie came in later to urinate, Mrs Baker put slacks on her because her legs were cold. She finally accepted this, with protest. A little later, Lottie came back inside, before the others, with some summer beach toys, asking if they could go swimming. Then, immediately, she began asking for—and taking—crackers. When Mrs Baker said that that was all, they were going home for supper, she went right ahead taking more. When she was stopped, she cried.

Mrs Baker reported that after their supper Mr Baker came

in late for his dinner. She sent Lottie upstairs with Heidi to get ready for bed so that she could serve and sit with Mr Baker. Soon after, she heard Lottie screaming in the most piercing, continuous fashion. She went upstairs. Heidi claimed that she had just started to try to undress Lottie, that she hadn't even gotten near her. Mrs Baker told Lottie to stop; but she went right on. Whereupon Mrs Baker spanked Lottie very hard and long—longer and harder than she thought she should have—but she was furious at the screaming, feeling that this little one is so capable of using other means to make her needs known. Meanwhile, Heidi disappeared; she could not bear to look. Dorrie stood solemnly by, watching. Then she left too. Lottie was crying and saying, "Okay. Okay. I won't." And then, after it was all over, Mrs Baker washed her, undressed her, put her to bed, read to her, and sang to her. Lottie was sweet and in good spirits, saying all the usual things. She didn't remember that the song 'Blow ye winds' had been sung—right after it was sung—so she had it again. She asked about the Brahms lullaby: "Why do you say 'Lay thee down'?"—pronouncing it "lay-dee-down" as if it were a nonsense phrase. She gave the usual invitation to her mother to get into her pajamas and come to bed with her, and then the statement: "No, you have to do your work. You go to bed with Daddy and see his penis."

When Mrs Baker came to put Dorrie to bed, a little while later, Lottie was sound asleep (she has been going to sleep very promptly at night). Mrs Baker read Dorrie the daily chapter in *Mary Poppins*. Dorrie remarked to her, as she was being tucked in, that she (Mrs Baker) looked quite a bit like Mary Poppins. Mrs Baker took this to be a tactful, way of saying that Dorrie felt her mother had gone too far with Lottie; she had spanked her much too hard.

There are a few final incidents to report which illuminate some facets of Lottie's behavior of this period. In a curious manner, Lottie combines her concepts of punishment-and-reward and male-and-female within the framework of 'birthday party'. For Lottie, a birthday party is the celebration of femininity through feasting and gifts, given as a reward for good behavior.

One afternoon, Lottie and Dorrie quarrel with unusual intensity in the back seat of the car, returning from a shopping trip (29-30). Lottie sobs: "Dorrie can't come to my birthday party!" I try to comfort Lottie by assuring her that Dorrie will certainly come to her party (four months hence), thinking that Dorrie has threatened not to come. Lottie cries all the more, tears soaking her cheeks: "Dorrie *can't* come to my birthday party, because she's *bad*!" Lottie has taken over the older girls' practice of threatening not to invite someone to her party when she is angry or, conversely, extending the invitation as a precious gift to anyone she likes. In this instance she feels impelled to impose the sanction of withdrawing the birthday invitation because of Dorrie's bad behavior to her; however, the consequence, that Dorrie will not be present at her party, is unbearable.

Lottie is reluctant to attend Danny's birthday party a week later (31-32):

LOTTIE   Little boys don't go to birthday parties.
MOTHER   Oh yes they do. There'll be boys and girls at this party.
LOTTIE   Little boys don't go to birthday parties because they have a penis.

Mrs Baker says that they can and do go to parties. She goes on to tell Lottie that little boys have little penises and little girls have little vulvas; boys grow up to be men with big penises and girls grow up to be women with big vulvas. Lottie stays very close to her mother at the party, climbing over her lap and watching the proceedings. She keeps asking for food: "Where is the party?" Only when the birthday lunch is finally served does Lottie become animated and sociable, talking and eating voraciously.

A new night fear begins in February. There is a reference toward the end of January to Lottie's persistent fear of fire-engine sirens. She wakes up in the middle of the night calling loudly for her mother because she has heard a siren. But now, to the old fear of a loud noise, signifying fire damage, is added a fear of "biting" animals. Several times in February she awakens at night: "There are crabs in my bed!"

MARCH

In March there are just four nursery-school sessions (35 through 38). School is closed for the spring vacation during the last two and a half weeks of the month.

Before the thirty-fifth session Mrs Baker tells Lottie that her father will take her to school and pick her up, but that he cannot stay. Lottie objects: "Mommy should go; Mommy should stay; Daddy should stay."

MOTHER Daddy will take you and come for you. You will be fine.
LOTTIE I will cry.
MOTHER You don't need to cry.
LOTTIE Yes I will.
MOTHER If you need to cry, it's all right.

Lottie goes off gaily with her father, carrying a bag of small chocolate Easter eggs to distribute at school. Mr Baker tells Lottie again in the car that he will not be able to stay. As soon as they enter the schoolroom, Lottie turns and grabs her father's legs tightly: "Don't go. Don't go." He extricates himself from the vise and says firmly, "I must go." Lottie cries very hard in Miss Wilkins's arms. Mr Baker leaves quickly, and by the time he has walked out to the door with the window in the hall she has stopped. When Mr Baker comes to call for Lottie, Miss Wilkins reports that she has had a fine morning.

Driving to school for 36, Mrs Baker tells Lottie that she is going shopping with me. Again Lottie announces that she will

87

cry. I suggest that she really does not need to cry. Lottie insists that she will, all the while in a cheerful mood. She just barely carries out her threat, crying for only half a minute when her mother leaves.

Lottie is outdoors when we return. She dashes to the door when she glimpses her mother, calling out, "Mommy! Mommy!" Then, immediately, she returns to the playground. A few minutes later she comes inside. She goes right over to Eddie's sixteen-month-old sister and sits down with her on the floor, playing gently. This day Lottie brings home from school one of the hamsters, which is being loaned to Heidi. On the way home, Lottie has the hamster in the cage with her in the back. She eats marshmallows, left over from the bag she took to school. She chats vivaciously and mentions that she cried.

The hamster from school has a short, unhappy stay in the Baker home. The day after 36 Lottie asks Dorrie to take the hamster out of its cage. When Dorrie tries to pick it up, the hamster bites her finger. Dorrie comes to Mrs Baker with her finger dripping blood; Lottie and Caron follow closely behind. The bleeding is stopped with pressure and Dorrie has to have a booster tetanus injection. Lottie wants to go into the doctor's office with Dorrie. She cries bitterly when this is not permitted. And she keeps talking about the "shot in the fanny".

The girls come to my house for the afternoon. After a short time outdoors with the others, Lottie comes in by herself. She has a quiet interlude with Caron's doll, fixing the doll carriage, wheeling it around the house, all the while talking sweetly and softly in her special high voice to the doll. Then Lottie plays again a game she invented a few days before. She goes to the cupboard under the sink and calls out: "There are biting dogs in there!" I say: "Just pretend." Lottie: "Oh no. *Really*." She flings open the doors: "See. There they are." She lifts out a large, empty ginger-ale bottle; it is one of the "dogs". This cupboard, used to store cleaning supplies, is one of the few places in the house forbidden to Lottie. Later in the afternoon, Dorrie complains more and more about her buttocks hurting from the injection. When she lies down on the couch Lottie wants to join her. Dorrie says that there is no room and Lottie cries until I find her another place on the couch. Dorrie talks about the pain when I bring the girls home. Lottie echoes Dorrie, most seriously: "Ohh, ohh, my fanny hurts. Ohh, I can't sit down"—moving as if in pain. When Dorrie goes to tell her father about it in another room, Lottie insists on going too. She tells him her finger hurts her. After he kisses it, she emerges smiling.

Once more, on the weekend, the hamster bites a member of the family. This time it is Mrs Baker who is bitten when she tries to handle it. So it is decided to return the animal to school. On the morning of 37 there is much talk on Lottie's part of not wanting to go to school. Mrs Baker is staying at home with Dorrie who is ill. However, reminded that the hamster must be taken in, Lottie goes cheerfully with her father. She tells him she will cry. He remarks that it is not necessary. And this time, when he leaves, she does not cry. When Mr Baker calls for Lottie he is told that she has had an enjoyable, no-crying morning. In the car Lottie says that she did cry. Mr Baker says he heard that she did not. As soon as they reach home, Lottie races up the stairs to her mother calling out: "I didn't cry! I didn't cry!" Lottie brings back with her a bright, quick, definite painting she has made. Several large, swirling, curving strokes of red, yellow, and blue intermingle in the lower right quarter of the paper.

On the final day of school before the spring vacation (38) Lottie is in a gay mood in the car with her mother and me. She has her bag of candy to distribute and makes her usual announcement that she will cry. When Mrs Baker leaves she gives only a token cry, lasting a few seconds. Later, Mrs Baker finds out, Lottie cries over a separate matter. Lottie does not want to give her candy to one of the girls, so Miss Wilkins gives out some school candy, but not to Lottie because she has her own. Lottie cries until Miss Wilkins—discovering what the trouble is —gives her a piece of school candy too.

Lottie greets her mother brightly outdoors at the end of the morning. She takes the jelly beans Mrs Baker has brought for her and hands them out to the children, especially to Timmy, who follows her everywhere, eager for more. Lottie plays with Eddie's little sister, and she swings. An assistant teacher reports that Lottie has played a lot by herself during the morning, not needing Miss Wilkins very much. She was on the swing alone for a long time and then went with Timmy on the double swing, laughing and talking.

At home during the first week of March (35 and 36) Lottie shows both unusually destructive and unusually self-destructive behavior. She hits herself between the eyes on the piano bench. She gets burned on the leg with an iron at the dressmaker's and then pulls off the blister. She bangs Heidi's mirror, breaking it. Other things are broken also. During this time she frequently wants to be like a baby, being particularly floppy and cuddly after the bath. This brief increase in concurrent destructive and baby-like behavior flares up at home at the same time as Lottie is finally achieving independent acceptance and enjoyment of school.

The pre-breakfast fights between Lottie and Heidi continue into March, about half the mornings. They most often concern what Lottie is to wear and whether or not she should get dressed. Heidi follows her mother's instructions doggedly, while Lottie balks and ends by screaming. Mrs Baker talks with Heidi: Lottie can only take orders from one mother; Heidi must be the big, sweet sister; Lottie *is* hard to manage and Heidi should come to Mrs Baker for help when Lottie is unmanageable. Perhaps here is the clue to this reaction of Lottie's. She may be displacing some of her angry feelings—too dangerous to express directly against her mother—onto her older sister, who sometimes carries out Mrs Baker's directions so inflexibly.

Another direct instance of Lottie's ambivalence to her mother and a displacement reaction, this time to me, occurs during the spring vacation. Lottie is in the kitchen with a large basket over her head singing: "I love you. I love you, Mommy." Mrs Baker says, "I love you, Lottie." Then Lottie sings: "My bunny lies over the ocean. Oh bring back my bunny to me." She plays on the floor with the basket of toys, with a puzzle, and with varied-colored nuts on a bolt, unscrewing them and naming all the colors, except grey, correctly. Suddenly, Lottie climbs on the stool under the birdcage and swings the cage violently. Mrs Baker gives her a spank and holds her tightly: "You may *not* do that—I've told you many times—that frightens the bird. He might die. Do you understand?" Lottie stands still and serious, not crying: "Yes." Then she comes directly over to me and bites my skirt.

By mid-March Lottie has added something new to the bedtime routine—her own version of the 'Don't-let-the-bedbugs-bite' rhyme: "Good night. Sleep tight. *Don't let the big girls bite.*" The occasional night fears persist and expand in content. The day following 38, Lottie wakes up twice in the night, crying and calling for her mother. The first time there are "crabs in my bed". The second time she complains of something on the ceiling. Mrs Baker lifts her up to show her that it is just the nursery birds hanging from the ceiling fixture. A few days later Lottie asks me if Caron has crabs in her bed. Twice in the following week Lottie wakes up saying there are owls going hoo-hoo, crabs, and snakes. She goes back to sleep after being reassured by her mother. Dorrie has been teasing and scaring her about owls, which are for Dorrie, too, something frightening: "An owl will come and go hoo-hoo," says Dorrie. Lottie has seen pigeons lately and heard them coo, a sound similar to the owl-cry she and Dorrie use. Both a crab and an owl appear in one of Lottie's favorite books, *I can fly*.

Lottie herself hints, in a joke, at what may be the latent meaning of her preoccupation with and fear of biting. She comes into the living room (in the third week of the vacation) and announces that she is going to ride on her dog. "I better not," she adds humorously, "he might bite my vulva!" This suggests that Lottie has developed a fantasy explanation of her lack of a penis: it was bitten off. If the associations are followed, the agent is variously named as dog, crab, owl, bedbug, big girl—pointing possibly to the ever-unnamed: Mother.

Whether or not this interpretation of Lottie's current fears, preoccupations, and discontents is correct, it is clear that she has reached a new developmental stage. Lottie is no longer the little girl that she was when school opened in the autumn. Then, at two years and three months, she was still bound to her mother in a close, unbroken attachment from babyhood. Now, at two years and nine months, she has discovered male and female and her place in this dichotomy. In this newly differentiated world, her father has become important and the old relationship to her mother less exclusive and more manifestly ambivalent. It is quite possible that this loosening of the infantile tie to the mother is necessary before school separation can be coped with—that is, accepted both realistically and without excessive suffering.

In any case, the main currents that move Lottie at this time flow, unabated, during the latter half of March when there is no school. School is no longer a major source and arena of disturbance and battle. The wide fluctuations of mood persist. Lottie is "impossible" at times, complaining, discontented, and provoking. Then the sun comes out from behind the clouds, she is gay, cooperative, helpful, and active. Her greatest dissatisfaction is still expressed in the clothing area. Food is a secondary target. For example, on the last day of March Lottie sleeps at naptime. She is very irritable when she awakens. Nothing is right. She wants neither to stay in bed nor to get up. Mrs Baker and I finally get her dressed, with Lottie complaining all the while about what she is wearing, her shoes hurting, and so forth. In the kitchen, getting a drink, I pour "too much". Lottie insists that it must be poured back and that *I* must get the juice bottle, not Mommy. Finally, Lottie goes outdoors to join Dorrie, Caron, and a group of neighborhood children. A few minutes later she reappears to get lollipops to distribute. She is now in fine spirits.

Lottie has become a teller of jokes; she has taken over some that Dorrie brings home from school. With apparent understanding and enormous relish, Lottie snares her victims again and again. The first joke of this genre seems to be an infinite source of satisfaction. "Do you know what?" she asks. "No. What?" you say. "That's what!" she shouts triumphantly. Her repertoire includes a more complex joke with a double punchline: "Is your refrigerator running?" "Yes." "Then hurry up and catch it. It's going down the street!" If you answer no to the same question, the retort is made: "Then hurry and get it fixed. The food will spoil!" Lottie still loves to sing "Oh, they don't wear pants on the sunny side of France." She is often heard humming the tune loudly. When her birthday is mentioned in passing, Lottie remarks again: "Little boys can't come to my party. They have a penis." Mrs Baker says that her daddy will come. Lottie laughs about her father coming to her party with his penis. Two days before, on an excursion to a farm with her family and mine, Lottie stands transfixed and fascinated at a fence, watching a herd of cows in the meadow. She comments: "They can't come to my birthday party because they make BMs outside." The cows moo and come over to the fence. Lottie does not want to leave.

There have been frequent discussions throughout March of the Baker family's vacation trip to Washington, D.C., planned for the first week in April. Mrs Baker gives Lottie the choice of going on the trip or staying with me. Without hesitation Lottie replies, "Washington!"

A few days before the trip, I take Lottie with Kaye to the latter's orthodontist. In the office Lottie is excited, curious, and friendly. She investigates everything, opening all the drawers, drinking at the fountain. She makes friends with everyone. In the car she tells me that she is going to Washington and after that: "I'm going to nursery school and I won't cry any more."

VII

Spring and Year's End

"I'm going to nursery school and
I won't cry any more."

Lottie became a schoolgirl at last in the spring. Each day she went eagerly to school, parted easily from her mother, and was reluctant to leave at the end of the morning. In this chapter the April and May material from school and home will be discussed first, followed by the June interview with Lottie's teacher.

Lottie attended thirteen of the seventeen spring sessions of school from 39 (9 April 1957) through 51 (23 May 1957). There were six school mornings for Lottie in April; she was away for the first two sessions on the week's vacation with her family and she missed one morning of the third week because of a cold. She was present at seven of the eight school sessions in May; illness kept her at home on the final day.

Lottie far surpasses expectations on the trip to Washington, D.C., with her family. She adapts well to strenuous sightseeing and a highly irregular schedule. At those times when she seems unable to take another step and has to be carried, some refreshment or a change of pace will renew her and she is ready to go on. Lottie even accompanies her family into the House and the Senate, solemnly promising to be quiet, and she does remain absolutely still. At the zoo she is unafraid of the huge animals; she wants to climb in with the elephants. But in the Botanical

Gardens she is upset by tiny ants. She notices each one and follows it anxiously: "Should I kill it or not? Dorrie, step on it! It will bite me!" All insects evoke concern and incessant talk.

At meals she hardly seems to eat at all; her main nourishment is orange juice. She sleeps well in a room with her sisters, despite different bedtimes and lights turned on. The lobby of the hotel is her own private preserve. She comes in, dropping her things all around, and stations herself at the small pool of water fed by a fountain. For all her complaining at home about footgear, Lottie does not even murmur one rainy day when her feet are soaked for hours, through a hole in her rubbers. Lottie writes a postcard to Miss Wilkins, scribbling it herself. She objects to her mother writing anything on it, agreeing only reluctantly to the necessary "Love, Lottie" which will enable her teacher to identify the sender.

At the end of March, it will be remembered, Lottie said that she would not cry any more when she returned to nursery school. Whether this was a prediction or a promise, Lottie is true to her word. She is excited and happy about going back to school. On the way (39) Mrs Baker mentions the many errands she has to do while Lottie is in school. Lottie bounds into the building in high spirits. At the door of her room Mrs Baker says, "Open it." "It's too hard," replies Lottie, suddenly grabbing hold of her mother's skirt. She clings, dragging along as they enter. There is a warm greeting from Miss Wilkins, who thanks Lottie for the card. Lottie is showing Alice the small toy animals she has brought, while Mrs Baker tells Miss Wilkins she will leave to do some shopping. From the midst of apparently absorbing play, Lottie rushes to her mother: "Don't go! Don't go!" There are a few sobs, but Lottie does not actually cry. Mrs Baker leaves and Lottie recovers immediately.

It was an excellent morning for Lottie, Miss Wilkins reports to Mrs Baker on her return, and it was the first day that all twelve children were there with no parents staying at school. On the drive home Lottie says that she cried at school. Mrs Baker replies

95

that she wouldn't call that real crying, Lottie has done very well.

Before the next session (40) Lottie is again told Mrs Baker's plans for the morning. She accepts them and does not cry when her mother leaves.

Lottie is outdoors on the teeter-totter with big Alice and she keeps right on swinging when Mrs Baker and I arrive to pick her up. Miss Wilkins says that Lottie has had a quiet, good time in school; she was involved in many things by herself, such as looking at books during music. Lottie is very disappointed at having to miss the next school session because of a cold.

By mid-April the final transformation of Lottie into a school-girl is completed. Home and school have converged into one world; now, within that world, they can be redifferentiated. For at this time, so firmly established is Lottie's acceptance of school, that it remains unaffected by immediate, disturbing home experiences. The death of a pet, or a quarrel with her mother, does not re-evoke anxious separation behavior. Lottie goes off eagerly each morning, no matter what has occurred at home. In fact, it could be said that school has taken on an independent function for Lottie: it has become an oasis, so to speak, to which Lottie goes twice a week and there refreshes herself.

At home, just before 41, the demise of a tiny kitten confronts Lottie, for the first time, directly with death. It brushes by her lightly; she is not yet ready. (However, only four months later, when her dog is killed, the realization of death will strike home.) Three kittens were born to the Baker cat on the day before the family's return from Washington. Now eleven days old, they have been inspected daily in their closet box and played with under supervision. The two "boys" have grown strong, but the minute "girl" hardly nurses at all, lies often in a corner by herself, and is one-quarter her litter-mates' size. This morning, during the before-school rush, Dorrie reports that the kitten is sleeping "funny". A few minutes later Lottie brings it in: "See, she's sleeping." It is stiff. They all gather around. Mrs Baker tells them that the kitten is dead. Lottie says, "I touched it." Her mother assures her that it does not matter, she has touched it too.

Dorrie is wide-eyed, Heidi concerned. Mr Baker comes in; he tells them about the survival of the fittest and the laws of nature. Mrs Baker reports that she herself was the most disturbed. Lottie, she feels, did not seem very upset.

On the drive to school (41) with her mother and me, Lottie is singing—lively and cheerful. "I won't cry," she announces. But when we park outside of school, she says, "Maybe I will cry." She runs into the building, opens the door of the room by herself, and enters without hesitation. She is greeted by Mrs Zerber. Even though Miss Wilkins is not there, Lottie does not cry when her mother immediately leaves.

She shouts a greeting to Mrs Baker from the teeter-totter, where she is swinging very fast with little Alice, when we come for her. There are many "tricks" she must do before she is willing to leave. She climbs to the middle of the teeter-totter and stands there singing; she insists on a final swing by herself. At last, with her painting and Jeanie, she goes to the car. The ride begins happily with Lottie and Jean clearing out the back seat. But later, Lottie wants Jean to move away from the middle of the seat and pushes her. When Jean pushes back, Lottie cries. Not consoled by a lollipop, she wants matzos. I offer a piece; she demands a *whole* one. I continue to offer the piece, which she solemnly refuses. However, a few minutes after, she reaches out and takes it.

Mrs Baker does not bring up her morning plans before the next session of school (42). She feels that Lottie is now able to accept going to school as a routine; the details of her mother's activities may just raise questions for Lottie about the parting. Lottie's entrance is gay and unhesitating. Miss Wilkins is back. Lottie turns to her mother: "Can you stay?" When Mrs Baker answers "no", it is accepted. And Lottie has a good morning. In the following session (43) the pattern is repeated: Lottie goes eagerly, parts without difficulty from her mother, and has a fine morning.

Before school on the last day of April (44) Mrs Baker warns Lottie to be careful not to step on the sweaters that are drying on the floor. A little while later she finds Lottie stamping on them and, thereupon, spanks her. However, when the time comes, Lottie leaves cheerfully for school with her father. When Mrs Baker, Caron, and I arrive at school, she is planted at the fish-bowl with both hands in the water, trying—without success—to catch the goldfish. Even though she is the last child left at school, she does not want to leave. But she finally comes away with her two paintings: one all green, covering almost the entire paper; the other having a few sparse, curving strokes on one part of the sheet.

At home, the concerns and complaints of the winter period continue during April. A new fear appears; a new skill is acquired.

Lottie awakens in the middle of the night before 42, calling out: "Crabs in my bed! Fire engines!" Toward the end of the month, Lottie initiates the bedtime enumeration of her main fears: crabs, fire engines, and owls. Her mother responds firmly: "There are *no* crabs in your bed. There may be a fire engine coming, but it's good because it goes to put out fires. Owls do *not* come inside the house, they live outdoors." Lottie still repeats as part of the night ritual: "Good night. Sleep tight. Don't let the big girls bite."

Lottie goes with her sisters for their third polio injections. She tells her mother: "I don't want the shot in my vulva." (A few weeks before she had a booster injection in her buttocks.) Mrs Baker assures her that it will be given in her arm. She enters the doctor's office without hesitation and only cries out at the time of the injection.

With the warm weather has come a revival of Dorrie's and Caron's fear of bees. They talk about it constantly and display extreme avoidance behavior with regard to these insects. Lottie has taken on their fear. One morning, in the last week of April, Lottie is playing alone in the back-yard. Mrs Baker hears "blood-curdling" screams; she is certain that only something disastrous could elicit such a sound and, for a moment, she is "paralyzed". Then she rushes out and finds Lottie (who stops screaming when she sees her mother) standing in the garage: a bee is flying around in there. Mrs Baker tells her that she could come inside the house or walk away from the bee—the bee is busy working—it is more scared of her than she is of it and bees rarely sting. But a few days later the alarming screams are heard again, in the same circumstances.

Lottie continues to be complaining and finicky about clothes and food. She frequently expresses her dissatisfaction with clothing by alleging that "it hurts". At supper-time (the day before 43) Mrs Baker puts a platter of ham and chicken on the table. Lottie, almost crying, says over and over, "I want teak (steak)." Every night she demands "teak" for dinner. When her mother tries to help her with her slippers, she cries: "No. I don't want those. They hurt. I don't want any. There's a thread in there." The following evening she objects again to slippers and robe: "I'm too hot. I'm too cold. It hurts." Only when her father orders her does she go to get them, crying.

By mid-April Lottie has mastered Dorrie's tricycle. She barely reaches the pedals, even with large blocks strapped on, but she can ride fast and turn in a small space. She seems to be in complete control of her vehicle and gets great pleasure out of it. Often she speeds by, pedaling with just one foot. On the last day of April the girls find an old bike basket in the garage and Lottie insists that it be put on Dorrie's tricycle immediately. (She has been riding Caron's tricycle which has a basket.) In such situations she can tolerate no delay in the carrying out of her wishes. After listening to plans of postponement she will just repeat her request, over and over. At these times the adults who deal with her feel impelled to get angry, punish, or acquiesce in order to gain any peace.

Lottie has become a punster, like Dorrie, with sly delight in her prowess. Also, she tries now to spell her name: "L-O-T-T-U-v spells Lottie," she says.

The seven school sessions which Lottie attends in May (45-51) are all characterized by cheerful trips to school with either her mother or her father, immediate and casual partings, and reports by the teacher of a fine morning in school. The only difficulty

99

now comes in prying Lottie loose from school at the end of each morning. There are always so many more things she must do before she is willing to go home.

At home in May Lottie consolidates a schematized drawing of a person, which she usually does with crayon on 4" by 6" paper. First she draws a circle at the top of the sheet. If the ends do not meet, she discards the paper and begins again. She may make as many as five starts. Then, stiffly and carefully, three or four small, irregular marks are added within the head: these are the facial features. Next, from the center of the paper down, come two straight, long lines for legs, slightly angled out. These are separated from the head and do not touch each other. The arms are two shorter lines, drawn from the head level (but unattached) up and out. Sometimes Lottie scribbles between the legs for "clothes". One drawing that Lottie makes in this manner she calls Mrs Adams (the maid); she adds a short line, centered between the legs, saying it is "her vulva". That Lottie is still involved in mixed fantasies about her sex identity is evidenced by a remark she makes in late May. In the bathtub one evening she says, smiling, "I'm Irving (Caron's father)."

Lottie and Heidi continue to conflict over dressing, especially in the morning. No matter what Mrs Baker does to minimize the possibility, loud arguments and sometimes tears (Lottie's) occur. Heidi locks her door to the younger girls' room. But early every morning, while Dorrie is sleeping, Lottie knocks and Heidi lets her in. Then Lottie gives some reason why she will *not* wear either of the two alternatives her mother has put out for her. Heidi insists that she must. Thus the altercation begins. It is clear that Lottie seeks out these battles with her older sister.

THE LAST DAY

Lottie is not well enough to attend school for the final session of the year. Mrs Baker tells her that she cannot go and that it is the last day. Lottie is very upset at missing school. She exclaims: "Wilkins didn't tell me it was the last day!"

Mrs Baker says that Lottie can invite some of the children from school to her birthday party (two weeks hence). "I want them all!" she declares. That would be too many, her mother explains, Lottie must pick just a few children. Lottie names only two: little Alice and big Alice. (Mrs Baker thinks that it is too hard for her to choose among the others.) Her mother adds that they will invite Miss Wilkins for dinner soon:

LOTTIE	(*With a smile*) Wilkins can be the Mommy.
MRS BAKER	No. She will be our guest.
LOTTIE	(*As if acknowledging her teasing*) You're the Mommy.

They telephone Miss Wilkins. Lottie speaks with her, smiling: "Hello Wilkins. Uh-huh. Uh-huh. . . ."

These reactions give some indication of the strength that Lottie's positive attachment to her teacher and to school has acquired by the end of the year.

Mrs Baker tells Lottie that she will go back to school in the fall, after the summer is over. She will go three days a week. Most of the same children will be back and Mrs Zerber will be her teacher. But very little of this comes across to Lottie, her mother feels. And when I try to explain to Lottie, in a variety of ways, that my family and I will be leaving soon to spend a year abroad, there is the same lack of comprehension.

It appears that, despite Lottie's clarity about the present and her exceptional memory for the past, events in the future are as yet inconceivable. This holds not only for distant time but for the imminent future as well. Phrases like 'just a minute', 'in a little while', or 'soon' have no specific meaning for her. Lottie's marked impatience, while undoubtedly related to other factors as well, is surely bound up with this age-characteristic void in time conceptualization. She often cannot wait; postponement of gratification is equivalent to her request being denied. Lottie inhabits the two-year-old world of here-and-now which is governed by a single time principle: now-or-never.

H

INTERVIEW WITH LOTTIE'S TEACHER

After the close of nursery school (10 June 1957) I interviewed Miss Wilkins, Lottie's teacher, on Lottie's behavior in school, her adjustment difficulties, and various methods of handling separation from the mother at nursery school. The following is a detailed record of the interview:

Miss Wilkins pointed out an important and special aspect of school for Lottie: the investment it had from Dorrie and Caron, and her mother's preparation for it. This led to both positive and negative effects. School meant something to Lottie in other relationships; she wanted Dorrie's school experience, not knowing what her own could be.

For Lottie, there was something that did not hold for any of the other children (she was the *only* youngest child in the group)—nursery school involved a special trip with her mother, just for Lottie. She had her mother on two special counts: first, her physical presence for school, and second, her mother all to herself. Lottie's holding on to her mother after a certain point (following Christmas and into February) was working out something with her mother, no longer having to do with school.

Lottie is very tenacious. She held on to things tightly— her mother and her teacher. At the beginning of the morning she held on to her mother. At the end of the morning she always had to hug her teacher tightly. To the very end there was this physical contact at departure, a tight hug.

She was affectionately hostile to her teacher and to her mother. Lottie holds, burrows in a cuddly, grabbing way; she lets go in a tight grip. She had angry feelings at her teacher for taking her away from her mother, and angry feelings against her mother for leaving her. Then, by the end of the year, it was the reverse—not wanting to leave her teacher and school. People are more important to Lottie than things.

Lottie is a tease. This was probably learned in part from

Dorrie. She *almost* gave a pinch or a bite to her teacher. She showed some rough affection to children, too. But with children she controlled much of her impulse to express anger. Sometimes she is a very angry little girl, wanting to hurt. Lottie probably will not ever be a real biter. Perhaps, now that she bites occasionally, some of her fears will go— although she is probably anxious at her own biting.

Lottie loved the hamsters; they were very exciting to her. She was very rough with them. She almost bit them a few times when kissing them. Her excitement was very marked —jumping and squealing.

Lottie showed anger in the use of her hands. She seemed to say: 'I could make this hurt if I let myself.' She wants to be caught in it and stopped. She is the great tantalizer. Once, when standing on a box outside where a leaf was hanging down within reach, Lottie said to Miss Wilkins: "I'm going to pull that! I'm going to pull that!" Miss Wilkins replied, "You can if you want." Then Lottie called out to Mrs Zerber: "I'm going to pull that!"

She started threatening her teachers early in the morning: "I'm not going to wear my sweater." Once, Miss Wilkins brought her sweater outside because it was cool and she asked Lottie to wear it. Lottie said: "I don't want my sweater. I need my sweater." She was caught in her own dilemma.

Lottie didn't really use school until her mother was out of the situation. Then she felt quite relieved of having to do anything. She was quiet, but responsive—a very different kind of person for four or five sessions. Then she became more active, painting and dancing. Lottie was interested in dancing in the beginning, then gave it up (many children did this), then came back to it. She also engaged in dramatic play in the doll corner.

At the end of the year Lottie went outside early, had juice and crackers very early, and then came in for a story or the phonograph. There was more organized indoor play at the end of the morning, and she went back to music. In music,

Lottie got pleasure out of the activity of jumping, running, and rolling on the floor. Her physical teasing was not with the children, but with the adults and the hamsters. Some children used music-time for physical contact and teasing but this was not Lottie's main use of dancing.

Not very much went on with other children. There was some dressing up and going places with neckties and hats, which were part of the housekeeping corner. Other children were there, but how important they were to Lottie is hard to say—they had no roles together, but they were *there* together. If one left the corner, the others tended to follow.

Lottie had a real relationship with June. June was also with Miss Wilkins a lot, so the two were together often. In the fall Miss Wilkins had thought them congenial, but it didn't take. Then, at the end of the year, it did. June, Lottie, and little Kaye were on Miss Wilkins's lap a lot. Little Kaye was the most independent of the three.

Lottie held a grudge. When you denied her, you had to re-establish the relationship before things were all right again. An example of this was a party at school with cup-cakes with marshmallow icing. June disliked marshmallows, so Miss Wilkins gave her a lollipop. The children were irate; there were no more lollipops. Miss Wilkins told a story about it and explained it. Lottie really wanted that lollipop. After finishing the lollipop, June ate the underside of a cupcake (which was very fine for her). This was the last straw for Lottie—and a few of the others. Miss Wilkins told Lottie all over again: if she had more lollipops, she would give them, but there were no more. Then Lottie was all right. She had been kicking her chair, crumbling her own cup-cake. Some of these incidents happened after her mother had left, later in the morning, and perhaps were partly a reaction to separation.

There is enough in Lottie to more than aspire to mature behavior; she can often attain it. She cannot sustain it at all times, however, and she is not comfortable within herself with dropping-back behavior. Except for crying—being a baby, being comforted—then she could give rein to less mature behavior. Crying gave Lottie great relief. It was the emotion unadulterated.

Lottie's urge for mastery (of techniques and materials) did not come through so much at school. Perhaps there was no need in school. She did work at puzzles and with the formboard (she solved it intellectually). But she worked hardest on relationships with people.

Mrs Zerber was accepted by Lottie, but not with the same intensity as Miss Wilkins.

Lottie remained very bothered by flies. Several other children were, also.

Hardly audibly, Lottie muttered in school: "Daddy has a penis." She showed much little-girl excitement over little boys going to the toilet. She would stand clutching her dress up to herself, but not at the toilet; it was not an imitation of boys urinating. There was more fantasy than acting out. She followed everyone into the lavatory, girls and boys. She was an exited toilet flusher (it was possible to flush the toilets continuously). This was stopped after a while. There was a lot of going to the toilet; Lottie had great control, enough to go often. She went with Mona to the toilet, sat (without urinating), pulled up her pants, put paper in and flushed it. There was sensory pleasure in sitting in the toilet and getting their buttocks wet. The children could lower themselves down to the water.

In her future nursery-school experience Lottie will be a good player, with much dramatic play. Perhaps it will be hard for her to change over to Mrs Zerber next year, because of her close relationship to Miss Wilkins. But she knows and accepts Mrs Zerber.

Lottie showed a great deal of teasing behavior over what she was going to eat and not eat—sand, pebbles, and dough of all kinds. She said: "I'm going to eat it!" (implying 'I'm not supposed to'). Miss Wilkins would say it wasn't tasty.

Lottie: "I'm going to! I'm going to!" There was not much *doing*, but much *baiting*.

When Miss Wilkins came to Lottie's house for supper (6 June 1957) Lottie made a big point about her glasses: she wanted Miss Wilkins to take them off and behaved as if she had never seen them before. Yet Miss Wilkins wears them constantly and Lottie has never seen her without them. Lottie looked through them, from behind. Perhaps the bifocals were confusing and when she looked into them they became something new, something else.

Miss Wilkins suggested an explanation for Lottie's prolonged difficulty in separating from her mother at nursery school: there were so many mother figures for Lottie (her own mother, myself, her two sisters, and Kaye and Caron) —such a large female group—all treating her with love, respect, and care, and all handling her similarly, that her relationship to her mother may have been less clear cut; or, she may have had more of a need for a *special* relationship with her mother, as at nursery school.

Miss Wilkins discussed some general observations about children's attitudes toward separation from the mother. The initial departure is acceptable when the mother is going out to do something for the child, such as buying him something or even shopping for food for the family. Then, when the mother goes *home*, that is not acceptable right away; the child must work it through. In the juice-time conversations the children knew where their mothers were. The light dawned: 'Mother is home, but I am here.' They *have* to know where their mothers go.

This was a very sympathetic group of children. They took things to Kent when his father left, he cried so hard. The group played 'Simon says' near him. If they were given lollipops, they gave theirs to Kent. One day, after Kent had cried, a child came to him later and asked: "Are you all right?"

An interesting incident happened with the group. One

day Miss Wilkins came in late, from a meeting. The children had been sitting at tables with puzzles and dough, with Mrs Zerber and an assistant. When Mrs Zerber left for a few minutes, the assistant noticed that the children stopped using their hands. When Miss Wilkins came in and sat at the table, their hands were busy again.

The mother's investment at the beginning of nursery school is so important; the child's capacity to do things, to use objects, is so tied up with his relationships to people. The mother being there—watching, seeing, and approving—is a way of introducing and accepting the child in nursery school; it means to the child that he *can* do things in school.

Miss Wilkins compared different methods of handling separation of the two-year-old from his mother in school. In another nursery school, after four sessions a member of the family other than the mother must bring the child. In that school the teacher-child relationship is paramount and not to be interfered with by the mother-child relationship. It works, but at what cost? On the other hand, at this school (Miss Wilkins's) the teacher tries to be a *teacher*, to have a new relationship with the child. It makes for a more serious problem, more serious children, and more negative behavior—but *trust* is maintained. The problem is faced. When it is solved, a good pattern is set up of school acceptance, separation acceptance, and a relationship with the mother on a new, more mature level. These children, by the third school year, are completely comfortable in school and can work out their school problems in school. A four-year-old who enters at four never shows the same complete comfort at the end of one year as those who have been there for three years.

It would be possible to handle separation by heroic distraction and interest techniques (e.g. a continuous succession of lollipops and all kinds of other props) but, instead, the problem is faced directly. For example, when Kent was very unhappy, Miss Wilkins offered him the kaleidoscope he had been interested in the week before: "Do you remember this?" Kent replied, "I remember *Mommy*!"

DISCUSSION OF TEACHER'S INTERVIEW

In the above interview Lottie's experienced teacher presents Lottie as she appeared in school. No attempt is made to give a comprehensive description. Rather, Miss Wilkins discusses Lottie as one child in her group of twelve two-year-olds. The most salient features of Lottie's school behavior are emphasized.

It may be useful to compare the two perspectives of Lottie that we now have: one, her school behavior as described by Miss Wilkins; the other, her behavior as observed in the home. One is struck immediately by the number of parallels.

"Tenacious" is the word for Lottie. "Affectionately hostile" to her mother and her teacher, she—literally and figuratively—holds on tightly to both.

Lottie is "the great tantalizer". She is constantly teasing and baiting her teachers about clothes, just as she does at home (threatening not to wear something needed), and about eating (threatening to eat something inedible). She wants to be caught and stopped.

"People are more important to Lottie than things." Lottie works "hardest on relationships with people"—predominantly with her teacher, for not very much develops with the children.

Lottie shows "much little-girl excitement over little boys going to the toilet". She follows everyone into the lavatory and is one of the most enthusiastic toilet flushers. She does not directly imitate boys going to the toilet—there is "more fantasy than acting out". She is heard to mutter: "Daddy has a penis."

The hamsters excite Lottie; when she plays with them she squeals and jumps. She almost bites them a few times as she is kissing them. Lottie is extremely bothered by flies at school, as are several other children.

Lottie can often attain mature behavior. She is uncomfortable within herself when she cannot sustain it. Only in crying is she able to permit herself to slip back into baby-like behavior; for Lottie, crying is "the emotion unadulterated".

Thus it is clear that many of Lottie's major characteristics are manifested both in school and at home: the constant baiting (especially in the areas of clothing and food); the overall tenaciousness; the importance of people (primarily mother and teacher); the mixture of affection and hostility in feelings; the striving toward mature behavior and the inner unacceptability of younger-level behavior (except for crying); the fear of insects; and the excited concern about sex differences.

We turn now to divergences between school and home behavior. Lottie is described at school as sometimes a very angry little girl. At home, on the other hand, she seems to show constant dissatisfaction rather than anger. Was she more angry at school, or could this be an artifact of her teacher's observational skill (e.g. the anger in the use of her hands)? If anger did come through more directly at school, was it a result of separation from her mother? Or, perhaps, was there greater freedom at school for Lottie to express angry feelings? Presumably she could not release anger as readily against her family at home, because of both internal and external restraints (with one exception: the quarrels with her older sister).

Lottie's sense of humor, the lighter side of her personality, does not stand out in this picture of her at school. (The extreme gaiety of the fall, as we have seen, was artificial and defensive.) It was evidently—and Miss Wilkins points this out—a very *serious* experience for Lottie to accustom herself to school, to build her attachment to her teacher, and to work through the problem of separating from her mother.

It would be expected that specific details of Lottie's fantasies might not be displayed at school. They involved primarily her rapidly changing relationship to her mother and father at home, influenced by her growing awareness of sex differences. It was primarily in the bedtime ritual, night fears, private games, and side remarks that they were revealed. Yet Miss Wilkins suspects that, after the Christmas vacation, Lottie "was working out something with her mother, no longer having to do with school". Further, her teacher notes the tendency to fantasy rather than acting out, in connection with Lottie's intense interest in boys going to the toilet.

Miss Wilkins's explanation of Lottie's prolonged difficulties in separating from her mother in nursery school suggests a factor that has not previously been considered: namely, that Lottie—because she was the youngest child in her family and was cared for by such a large group of mother figures (in her family and mine)—had a particular need for the special relationship with her mother that school afforded.

Certainly most observers would agree that two-year-olds have a great need for individual mothering. It may well be that nursery school, incidentally, can offer some children of two the opportunity to enjoy their mothers' presence, for a time, without the interference of siblings and a busy household. However, Miss Wilkins's conjecture is that only in school did Lottie have her mother entirely to herself. If Miss Wilkins's surmise were correct—that Lottie's separation difficulties could be ascribed to a relatively exceptional mother-child relationship characterized by a particular form of deprivation of the mother's individual attention—then the potential generality of this study would be extremely limited. That is, what we learn from this case would be applicable at best only to that small class of children who were deprived of their mothers' time except at nursery school.

From extensive home observations I see no basis for this view. Lottie's mother spent almost every morning alone with Lottie. Her sisters and father were sometimes at home for lunch; but they soon left. Then Lottie remained with her mother for the early afternoon until the older girls came home from school after three. Moreover, Lottie and her mother had a quiet, private time together at bedtime every evening. Throughout the day Mrs Baker was available when Lottie showed signs of need. (The close relationship of the Baker family with mine does not alter this picture.) The overall impression is one of a normal mother-child relationship; there is certainly no deviation from what would be expected in any family with three children.

Hence, it seems very doubtful that Lottie's separation reactions and clinging in school resulted from a chronic hunger for being with her mother, stimulated by insufficient exclusive contact with her in the home. Therefore, we have some reason to expect that the factors making for separation difficulties in this study will not be highly unusual.

Miss Wilkins observes that "Lottie didn't really use school until her mother was out of the situation. Then she felt quite relieved of having to do anything." Her teacher reports Lottie as being a very different child for several sessions—quiet, but responsive. Following this period, she became more active, resuming painting and dancing.

It may have been that Lottie experienced a sense of relief, when she first stayed independently at school, from the urgency of doing things, of keeping up, which was certainly a constant force that drove her within her family. Perhaps—even though she was now ready to stay without her mother—it was, also, a solemn step to have taken, requiring a new assimilation of school in these new circumstances. Then school could become her own, a place without mother.

VIII

Discussion and Conclusions

SCOPE OF THE STUDY

To investigate the detailed reactions of a young child to an initial recurrent, routinized separation from the mother, a two-year-old child was studied at home and at school during her first year at nursery school. The investigator's friendship with the child's family and the mother's full cooperation facilitated collection of the study material. The data consisted of: (1) numerous direct observations by the investigator of the child in the home (several each week); (2) reports by the mother on every nursery-school session, outstanding emotional events in the life of the child, and changing patterns of home behavior throughout the year; and (3) an interview with the nursery-school teacher at the end of the year on the child's behavior in school.

The child, Lottie, was chosen for study not only because of the rare opportunity to investigate home behavior, but also because the school separation occurred under optimum conditions. Lottie—a normal, highly verbal child—was the youngest of three girls in a professional, middle-class family. She was two years and three months at the start of the study; she reached three years of age by its close. Her parents, intelligent and sensitive to the needs of their children, were aware of the possibility of separation difficulties and they tried to minimize them for Lottie. She had not been exposed to any extreme separation experiences in the past. Also, the nursery school had a policy of gradual adaptation to maternal separation, accepting the mother's presence until the child seemed ready to stay alone. Moreover, the program for two-year-olds comprised only two mornings of school each week. These benign circumstances served to reduce the chances that traumatic handling of separation could account for the reactions.

There are three contributions an individual case study can make: (1) As 'natural history' it can increase understanding of the complexity and variation of human behavior, by detailed exemplification. (2) It can illuminate psychological processes that mediate relationships between variables which have already been investigated. And (3) it is a source of new hypotheses concerning relationships between variables that remain to be studied systematically. The second and third functions of the case study will be emphasized as much as possible in the following discussion and summary.

The hypotheses derived from and suggested by the study will be organized within the phases of the child's developing separation reactions. Some of the statements show relationships involving intra-personality variables that may be age-specific or limited to one particular type of child. An effort is made, however, to highlight hypotheses that seem likely to be more general in scope. Only further research—controlled studies with groups of children—will determine their validity and their limiting conditions.

CASE SUMMARY AND HYPOTHESES

Inordinate Defenses

When Lottie's mother left her for the first time in nursery school on the third morning, Lottie ran to her locker and stood there, laughing, calling out over and over the names of the members of her family: "Mommy! Daddy! Dorrie! Heidi!" Lottie was on her teacher's lap and turned briefly away from her mother when she returned only a few minutes later.

Left by her mother in an alien place, Lottie loudly invoked

113

the images of her family. In her months-long efforts to cope with separation from her mother in school, Lottie was a two-year-old who struggled and at times showed her disturbance. She did not belong to that class of two-year-olds who are the chronic 'quiet ones', slipping quickly and easily into an apparently trouble-free acceptance of nursery school and mother separation.

In a private conversation in 1957 the late Dr Katherine Wolf discussed some of the possible dangers for the two-year-old starting nursery school. She pointed out that the "internalized mother image" was as yet not clearly formed; an apparently smooth acceptance of school and separation from the mother might involve a denial mechanism (the teacher "becoming" mother) resulting in a weakened, confused internal image with serious implications for future personality development. On the other hand, a two-year-old's manifest struggle and difficulties might be a "healthier" reaction. She felt that by approximately three years of age the situation changed, the mother image would be more strongly established and nursery-school separation from the mother would tend to be experienced with perhaps greater surface disturbance than is usual at two, but with less risk to the developing personality.

Many questions are raised by Dr Wolf's provocative remarks that warrant systematic investigation. Would a comparison of two-year-olds who maintain for several months a carefree acceptance of mother separation with those who overtly object yield evidence of personality damage to the former? Does the two-year-old have difficulty in maintaining a mother image in her absence and at what stage of development is an internalized mother image firmly established? Since Lottie became an objector, her case mainly illuminates some of the mechanisms involved in this particular type of reaction to separation. This study does reveal, however, several ways in which a child of two strives to keep the mother in mind during separation (one example being the naming device cited above).

It can be said, in retrospect, that Lottie was not ready for nursery school when she started in the fall at two years and three months of age. This is evidenced, not in the strenuous objections she later voiced to her mother's leaving her, nor in the half-year's time required for her to become a schoolgirl, but in the unexpected, extreme defenses that she resorted to during the first few months of school. These can be seen as attempts by the child to cope with a stressful situation that was overwhelming to her; through various forms of denial she tried to reduce the suffering and to find a short cut, as it were, to the easy acceptance of school and separation from the mother that was expected of her and that she wanted for herself.

Lottie's first exaggerated defense took the form of pseudo-elation. At the beginning, in school, she tried to laugh it off: in jokes, songs, and unnatural gaiety in situations calling for the reverse, she denied her need to cry, substituting laughter for tears. That this was denial through elation, rather than the start of a happy acceptance of school, is indicated by the exaggerated and transient nature of the hilarity and of the behavior which accompanied it. For, after about three weeks, she gave up this defense and, no longer buoyed by elation, became for a few sessions serious and restless in school.

Then Lottie fell back on her second and major line of defense: identification with her sister. From the start of school Lottie built up this defense; it developed concurrently with the pseudo-elation. Slips of the tongue, remarks, choice of clothing and activities—all testified obliquely to the increasing strength of the identification: 'I am not small, frightened Lottie going to nursery school—I am big, strong Dorrie going to kindergarten.' If she could not cope with nursery school as her small self (at home she was going around saying "I don't like my own self"), perhaps the shield of 'being Dorrie' was a necessary defense during the first difficult period at school, to enable her slowly to get used to the strange horde of children, the unfamiliar room, the different ways and routines of doing things; perhaps it made it possible for a relationship of trust to start between herself and her teacher.

Only briefly, for two or three sessions, did Lottie achieve a degree of self-reliance and contentment in school through this denial of herself and her own inadequacies. Then she stated openly: "I am Dorrie. Call me Dorrie"—and with this revelation of the defense came the beginning of its disintegration.

A relative absence of crying and other manifestations of negative affect does not necessarily imply that the young child is able to cope with separation from the mother: gaiety, behaving like an older child, or apparent acquiescence are likely to be based on denial defenses, which temporarily enable the child to ward off separation anxiety.

Temporary Defenselessness

It was as if Lottie were already giving up her defensive identification with her sister when she stated it in words and laid it open to reality and its inevitable rejection by her mother and teacher. Then, if Lottie could no longer 'be' her five-year-old sister Dorrie in school, she became herself—a two-year-old—disturbed and angry with this new school experience and with her mother for leaving her there.

Once bared, the sister defense began to crumble. There followed in the next four sessions the first direct provocation of the mother in school, increasing overt objection to separation and the onset of crying.

When Lottie first cried for her mother at school, it was a delayed reaction that came later in the morning after her mother had gone. Then, on the eighteenth morning of school, Lottie burst into tears at the moment of parting. It was after her mother's return in this session that Lottie, playing at her side, said: "This is not Dorrie's school. This is Lottie's school."

The final renunciation of her defense left Lottie vulnerable to the full impact of separation anxiety. Instead of the steady improvement that her mother had anticipated with Lottie's acknowledgement of nursery school as her own, Lottie's behavior deteriorated. She would not let her mother leave; she cried bitterly when her mother did go; she clung more and more to her mother at school, showing much less independence in her activities than before; her play was limited, regressed, and, at times, wild and destructive. At home she very briefly lost urinary control, wetting herself a few times after having been completely dry for half a year. Moreover, she showed increased longing for her mother during home separations.

This phase of the case study suggests: The stronger the denial defense that the young child is impelled to use in coping with separation from the mother, the greater will be the impact of separation anxiety when the defense is relinquished.

A Second Attempt

During the winter Lottie had to work through mother separation again. The outstanding features of the period were the absence of the exaggerated defenses of the fall and the far-reaching developmental changes within Lottie, related to her discovery of sex differences (see below).

This time—without the aid of extreme defenses and supported by the familiarity of her school surroundings and the established relationship with her teacher—Lottie seemed to start anew. Slowly, begrudgingly, but without much affect, she accepted her mother's leaving her at school for increasing periods.

Lottie's separation reactions followed a sequential pattern: reluctance and hesitation, holding on to mother, denial of parting, restraint of crying, return to crying, persistence of crying, and, finally, acceptance of separation with token tears.

Lottie needed to cry when her mother left her at school, but this she did not permit herself during the first winter month. Did Lottie withhold her tears because crying was associated with the breakthrough of her feelings of helplessness and rage that occurred when she had given up her major defense late in the fall? To cry, to feel again the direct impact of separation, was dangerous.

Once, however, that Lottie was able to cry again for her mother at the moment of parting, the crying pattern persisted. She talked about it continually. The recurrent January statement after every

I

school session, "I didn't cry" (signifying 'I didn't let myself cry'), gave way to February's invariable announcements: "I will cry" before school, and "I cried" after school. Lottie *did* cry every morning in school. Only in March did the crying dwindle to token tears. The one morning—her father had brought her to school—that there was no crying and no felt need to cry, she rushed upstairs to her mother on her return home, calling out: "I didn't cry! I didn't cry!"

Thus it appears that the young child must be free from extreme defenses and suffer through the experience directly before separation from the mother in school can be accepted on a sound basis.

Mother Separation from within

The new basis for Lottie's successful re-experiencing of school separation in the winter evolved out of significant developmental changes in her relationships to her parents.

Lottie, at two and a half, had moved from a primary relationship at home with her mother to a triangular one involving her father. She had become acutely aware of him and manifestly ambivalent in her feelings.

Lottie conflicted with her father at home as this difficult transitional relationship developed. She perceived him as the successful rival for her mother's love. The major preoccupations of the time concerned sex differences and body damage. There were increasing sex talk and frequent questions about sex; "penis" and "vulva" joined "BM" as favorite words.

Lottie became extremely meticulous, demanding, and dissatisfied about clothing. Her discontent with herself and her provocation of others were centered in this sphere. This restless dissatisfaction with body covering may have been an expression of Lottie's inner turmoil over the recent discovery of her own sex identity. The winter home pattern of 'controlled wetting' enabled her to imitate the masculine role in a feminine fashion and maximized the number of clothing changes.

Although in school Lottie did not manifestly employ the sister

118

identification any longer as a defense, at home it continued to flourish. This versatile identification apparently functioned now for Lottie as an aid in reconciling herself to femininity: 'If I could be (dressed like) Dorrie, then I could be content as a girl.'

New night fears appeared. To the old fear of fire sirens was added a fear of "biting" animals—crabs, snakes, and owls in her bed. She included her own version of the bedbug rhyme in her bedtime ritual: "Good night. Sleep tight. Don't let the big girls bite." In the morning battles over what she was to wear, she displaced her hostility toward her mother onto her older sister.

There are many indications that Lottie had developed a fantasy explanation of her lack of a penis: it had been bitten off. Further, the evidence hints that the unnamed agent was Mother.

Whether or not this interpretation of Lottie's fears, preoccupations, and discontents is correct, it is clear that she had reached a new developmental stage. At two years and nine months, Lottie had discovered male and female and her own sex identity; in this newly differentiated world her father had become important and the old relationship to her mother less exclusive and manifestly more ambivalent.

It seems probable that the loosening of the infantile tie to the mother is necessary before school separation can be coped with— that is, accepted realistically and without excessive suffering.

Acceptance of School

Lottie became a schoolgirl at last in the spring. Each day she went eagerly to school, parted easily from her mother, and was reluctant to interrupt her activities when it was time to go home. She was very attached to her teacher. There were regular reports of a fine morning. The only difficulty now came in persuading Lottie to leave school.

It had been a hard task for Lottie at the beginning of the year to merge home and school into one world. In April they could be redifferentiated within that world. For now, so firmly established was Lottie's acceptance of school that it could remain unaffected by immediate disturbing home experiences. The death of a pet or a quarrel with her mother did not re-evoke anxious separation behavior.

School took on, in the end, an independent function for Lottie. It became a place of her own, fulfilling needs and offering satisfactions away from home.

Future Time and Separation

Lottie at three years of age showed no comprehension of events in the future or of the duration of time. Now-or-never was the time principle governing her world.

There are many questions that call for systematic investigation in the area of time conceptualization. What is the normal sequence of time-concept acquisition in young children? At approximately what ages do the various stages occur? How do young children cope with the problems arising out of their inadequate understanding of time? In what ways does the child's conceptualization of time tie in with the capacity to wait for gratification, which is regarded as a crucial, developmental step in the psychoanalytic theory of the change from primary to secondary process?

It may be useful to consider some of the possible implications of a lack of future-time comprehension for the young child separating from his mother in school. He could not be *sure* that she would ever return, nor could he have the slightest notion of how *long* it would be. If 'the future' does not exist cognitively for a child, then he has no sense of the passage of future time, no means of estimating its duration, and no certainty of the advent of any given future moment into the present. Little wonder then, even setting aside the many other relevant factors, that the two-year-old may have difficulty in separating from his mother in nursery school. Brought to a strange place, left in the care of unfamiliar adults, surrounded by an alarming throng of unknown children—what help is it to him that his mother has said that she will be back soon? He is aware only of the disaster that has struck: his mother has gone.

Only when the alien place that school appears to be at first becomes transformed for the child into a familiar, safe place—only then can he part with ease from his mother. But this is not, I believe, because he has learned that his mother will unquestionably come back within a certain time period. Rather, he becomes willing to take his chances. He can gamble, so to speak, on his mother's return to school if he is quite accustomed to the children, the room, the yard, the toys, the routines, the activities, the patterns of the day—and, above all, if he is secure in his relationship to his teacher.

Furthermore, perhaps by the end of his third year, he may be capable of holding in his mind a fairly clear image of Mother during short absences, providing that he feels 'at home'—just as he can probably retain the mother image in his own home, where there are so many reminders of her presence.

The following hypotheses are suggested. When a young child is separated from his mother: (a) the more familiar he is with the place where he is left, the less the separation anxiety that will be evoked; and (b) the stronger the positive attachment to the person in whose care he is left, the less the separation anxiety that will be evoked. There are also some indications for an additional hypothesis: A crucial factor in establishing the young child's familiarity with new places and persons is repeated exposure in the presence of the mother.

If the foregoing hypotheses are correct, it follows that separation anxiety in young children may be minimized by allowing the child to become accustomed to the place of separation (the nursery school, the home of a friend, or any new surroundings) and to the person who will be in charge of him (the teacher or the baby-sitter) *in the presence of the mother, before the initial separation occurs.*

The long course of Lottie's adjustment to nursery school can be summarized from this point of view. Lottie began school at the age of two years and three months. She made, at first, several

unsuccessful attempts at a rapid solution of her separation difficulties through the adoption of exaggerated denial defenses.
Then Lottie kept her mother at school while she herself was
becoming thoroughly at home there and until it became possible
for her to release her feelings in crying. Concurrently she built
up a close attachment to her teacher, not relinquishing her
mother until she was sure of another adult in school. When all
these requirements were satisfied—that is, school had become
entirely familiar and permeated with her mother's presence, and
Lottie could express her feelings there in the care of a teacher
who was loved and trusted—then Lottie was able to bid farewell
to her mother lightly and to enjoy school fully. However, it
must be remembered that when this satisfactory state of affairs
was finally attained Lottie was two years and nine months old,
and she had reached a developmental level that may well be a
necessary condition for a sound acceptance of separation from
the mother in nursery school.

Major Hypotheses

In this chapter six principal hypotheses have been presented which
appear to warrant systematic investigation. They are reproduced
below as a summary statement of the main inferences drawn from
the case study:

1. A relative absence of crying and other manifestations of
negative affect does not necessarily imply that the young child
is able to cope with separation from the mother: gaiety, behaving like an older child, or apparent acquiescence are likely
to be based on denial defenses, which temporarily enable the
child to ward off separation anxiety.

2. The stronger the denial defense that the young child is
impelled to use in coping with separation from the mother, the
greater will be the impact of separation anxiety when the defense is relinquished.

3. The young child must be free from extreme defenses

and suffer through the experience directly before separation from the mother in school can be accepted on a sound basis.

4. The loosening of the infantile tie to the mother is necesssary before school separation can be coped with—that is, accepted realistically and without excessive suffering.

5. When a young child is separated from his mother: (a) the more familiar he is with the place where he is left, the less the separation anxiety that will be evoked; and (b) the stronger the positive attachment to the person in whose care he is left, the less the separation anxiety that will be evoked.

6. A crucial factor in establishing the young child's familiarity with new places and persons is repeated exposure in the presence of the mother.

7. As a corollary to hypotheses 5 and 6, the following lead concerning preventive policy is suggested: Separation anxiety in young children may prove to be minimized by allowing the child to become accustomed to the place of separation (the nursery school, the home of a friend, or any new surroundings) and to the person who will be in charge of him (the teacher or the baby-sitter) *in the presence of the mother, before the initial separation occurs.*

IX

Epilogue: the next six years

Lottie's development at home and in school was followed in the next six years by means of interviews with her parents, supplemented by direct observations. A few months before Lottie finished kindergarten (April 1960), Mrs Baker agreed to summarize some of the outstanding features of the intervening three years. Numerous home visits enabled me to observe Lottie's adjustment as a five-year-old. Although the Baker family moved to a distant city the following year, there were several reunions, and both parents were interviewed when Lottie was eight and a half (January 1963).

TWO MORE YEARS AT NURSERY SCHOOL

1 April 1960. Follow-up interview with Lottie's mother

LOTTIE AS A THREE-YEAR-OLD. Before school started, Mr and Mrs Baker took Lottie to a library very near the nursery school to show Lottie where her mother would be working while Lottie was at school. This plan was accepted by Lottie. When she showed some confusion, her mother restated the arrangement: "You go to your school and I go to my work. I will pick you up." Lottie never cried when her mother left her. Mrs Baker never stayed in school. (Mrs Baker had made up her mind that she would not send Lottie to nursery school that year if there were difficulties.)

Lottie was not always delighted to go to school. But she accepted going. Her mother had thought that she would shift her main attachment from Miss Wilkins to Mrs Zerber, the head teacher of the threes (who had been the assistant teacher in the two-year-old group). Instead, Lottie turned to the assistant teacher of the threes, developing a strong, warm relationship with her. (Lottie never replaced Miss Wilkins, in the sense that her main attachment, during each of the two subsequent years at nursery school, was with the assistant teacher.)

Lottie enjoyed large-muscle, outdoor activities the most: climbing, sandbox, jumping, and swinging. It seemed to be a year of settling down. There was more calmness, more observation than participation. At home, Mrs Baker recalled, Lottie showed somewhat less discontent. Her night fears continued for the first part of the year.

In the summer, before this second year of nursery school started, the Bakers' dog was run over and killed. The entire family reacted strongly to the death of the dog, including Lottie. After this happened there were many discussions with Lottie, and she asked numerous questions, about death. Lottie became very interested in cemeteries (there was a cemetery near her house). She asked where people go after they die. Can you see? Can you hear? She explored the subject, her mother remembered, to its fullest.

This was the year that I and my family spent abroad. Lottie did not want to talk about our absence or have it brought to her attention. She did not want to have our letters read (her sisters shared this reaction). Lottie, however, would actively sabotage the reading and have to be sent away. It was difficult to get the girls to write any letters, including Lottie. When Mrs Baker showed Lottie a picture of me, she would say while she was looking at it: "I can't remember what Margie looks like. I won't know her." But she did seem to know us very well on our return. A close relationship was immediately re-established.

LOTTIE AS A FOUR-YEAR-OLD. Lottie turned to her father with strong, positive feelings during this year.

There was a car-pool arrangement for driving to nursery school with another family. Lottie became attached to the other father who drove frequently. With his son, her classmate, she was domineering and motherly. There was no separation problem, although much discussion on Lottie's part about who was taking her to school and who was calling for her. This was a good year. Lottie was part of a group in school which comprised herself and her two best friends, Linda and Joan. Occasionally, other children were added. The major activities were in the doll corner, with peg-boards, and outdoor play. Lottie also painted many pictures, especially when Linda did. Her main adult relationship in school was again with the assistant teacher (not the same person as the year before).

A few days before Lottie's final day at nursery school, Mrs Baker took Lottie to register at the neighborhood public school kindergarten (where Dorrie had gone). Lottie met the teacher, played with the toys, and had a thoroughly enjoyable time. She wanted to start right away. Her mother had to explain that she would not be going to kindergarten until the fall, after the summer vacation.

KINDERGARTEN

The following material is taken both from the follow-up interview with Mrs Baker in April 1960 and from several direct observations which I recorded during the kindergarten year concerning specific reactions to school, separation experiences, and future-time comprehension.

The first morning of kindergarten lasted only half an hour. The mothers attended with their children. Afterwards I asked Lottie how it had gone. She replied, "*Perrrfect!*"

In January 1960 Mrs Baker reported on Lottie's adjustment

to school. She said that Lottie was dissatisfied with kindergarten. She did not behave very well. She did not "conform"
and she was "no star pupil". The restrictions and regulations
bothered her, especially the frequent standing in line and the
daily rest period in which no talking was permitted. Her
teacher (Miss Miller) was a gentle and kind person. (Dorrie
had also had Miss Miller in kindergarten.) But for Lottie, Mrs
Baker surmised, kindergarten was more like nursery school
than "real school" and yet it could not come up to nursery
school in any way. The highlight of a kindergarten morning was when Lottie caught a glimpse of Dorrie; her class-
room was in the same building. Dorrie, also, would report
with glee whenever she had seen Lottie in school.

One snowy January morning Mrs Baker was walking
home with Lottie from school. Lottie complained that
she was tired and she asked her mother to carry her. Mrs
Baker said that she could not do that any more—Lottie
was beyond that. Next year she would be in first grade.
She would go to school all day and learn how to read and
write. Lottie brightened up: "Yes. Then *they* won't be
able to whisper and talk above my head." Mrs Baker inquired
who "they" were. "Dorrie and Caron," Lottie replied,
"they read and write things and I can't understand. But I
will next year." Mrs Baker assured her that she would learn
to read and write. She added that it would take time. On
several occasions, while playing at my house with Dorrie
and Caron, Lottie had rushed out of the room, crying:
"They're telling secrets!" The older girls had denied this.
But they did use their superior knowledge to write messages
to each other from which Lottie was excluded. Apparently,
despite her mother's careful explanations, Lottie believed
fervently that she would learn to read and write immediately
on entering first grade: all at once, she would understand
everything. Meanwhile, Lottie was trying to learn how to
spell at home. She frequently asked to have words spelled

for her and she used her punning prowess to make words out of letters. A friend's name 'Emmy' she wrote "M E". She proudly showed a piece of paper on which she had written "Dorrie is P P".

Mrs Baker described one of Lottie's difficulties. She "hated" to have to *wait* for her mother, or another adult on whom she was dependent. She still talked about the one time in the fall that her mother had been late (six minutes) in picking her up at school. All of the other children had gone and Lottie had been waiting alone. After this she constantly worried about the possibility of her mother coming late for her at school. There were several other instances of this concern during the month. Lottie developed a close friendship with Meg, one of her classmates. But she almost decided not to go to Meg's birthday party because of the possibility that her mother might be late in calling for her—even though Meg's home and family were very familiar to her. (It is relevant here to note that Mrs Baker was generally extremely prompt.) Lottie did go to the party because, at the last minute, Dorrie was invited too. When Dorrie was present Lottie did not have the fear. (Mrs Baker believed that this reaction did not involve a reactivation of the two-year-old separation problem but was a new development; Lottie had fantasies of something bad happening to her mother if she were at all late.) Another incident occurred in school. One morning Lottie's teacher was a few minutes late: "I was alone with my thirty children!" Lottie exclaimed to her mother afterwards—and she kept retelling the story.

On a January night when her parents were out, Lottie had a conversation with me at bedtime:

LOTTIE   How old will Mommy be when I am eighty?
I   About one hundred and ten years old. But people don't usually live that long.

LOTTIE I wish people didn't die. I wish when they died,
they became little babies and started all over again.
They can't really.

During the kindergarten winter, the concern about waiting
for her mother seemed gradually to lessen. Although there
were signs in other areas as well that Lottie was less worried
about it, in part this resulted from her being permitted to
walk home from school by herself. She took great pride in
her independence and preferred to have no one come for her
at school. However, another difficulty arose in this period.
Lottie's frequency of urination increased markedly; it
reached an average of two or three times an hour in the day-
time. She would go to the toilet just before a meal or excursion, then *have* to go again a few minutes later. At first her
parents handled the situation with reassurance and assistance,
waiting for her and finding toilets whenever necessary.
However, it became apparent that Lottie was using the
urgency to urinate both to circumscribe her own activities
(choosing to stay at home) and to manipulate the family
(they *had* to wait for her, they *had* to stop the car to find a
bathroom). After a careful medical examination showed no
physical cause for the increased need to urinate, Lottie's
parents (at Mr Baker's insistence) instituted a different
approach to the problem. They imposed strict rules: Lottie
was *not* permitted to leave the table during meals; they
would *not* stop the car on short drives, and so forth.
Under this regime Lottie's urinary problem diminished.
There remained, by the spring of 1960, only a somewhat
greater frequency of urination (not extreme, however)
than before the onset and Lottie continued to take the pre-
caution of always using the toilet before leaving home.

It must be noted that Meg, Lottie's best friend from kindergarten with whom she often played after school, showed the
same continual need to urinate (before Lottie did). It is
possible that Lottie, for needs of her own, picked this up

from her friend. In late February Meg and her family moved away to another state. Lottie and Meg parted in tears. Lottie did not find a replacement for her friend in the following months. She spoke of Meg frequently with longing.

Lottie's first two report cards from kindergarten dismayed her sisters. There were many marks that were merely 'Satisfactory' or even 'Needs improving' both for her work and for her social behavior. By the third marking period (in the spring), however, Lottie showed great improvement. The work side was now filled with 'Outstanding'. The less satisfactory marks for social behavior, her teacher said, were almost entirely because of Lottie's inability to stop talking.

In her home activities Lottie started to play "little dolls" intensively and independently (a game in which she had participated with her sisters when she was two). Lottie showed me one of her set-ups in February: In "her" family, the mother was dead and the older sister took care of the little ones; part of her equipment included the doll-house which was being used as an "orphanage". Lottie also became an avid player of boxed games; she was very strict about the rules.

During a conversation at the dinner table on the subject of belief in God, each member of the Baker family spoke. When Lottie's turn came, she said: "I have a God. His name is *Daddy*."

It will be recalled that orange juice, which Lottie called apple juice, was her favorite drink from the time she was weaned until she reached three years of age. During the following year her preference shifted to the drink designated by the misnomer. Apple juice became and remained supreme. Before her fifth birthday Lottie repeatedly said: "When I'm five, I'm going to be good—except for drinking apple juice." She continued to drink it in large quantity and she took on the task of checking to see that the home supply was always ample.

Lottie rarely made such mistakes with words or had difficulty in remembering them. There were two singular exceptions: She could not remember 'Bermuda', the place to which her parents went without her for a five-day vacation when she was four years old; and at five and a half she kept forgetting the word 'Virginia' during the time her parents were planning to go there by themselves for a week's vacation.

In February 1960 Lottie showed an unusually strong reaction to a home separation under special conditions. When her parents left for the evening, they took Dorrie to a friend's house to spend the night. Lottie stayed with a baby-sitter, Gladys, whom she had requested. When it was time for Heidi to go to her social-dancing class for an hour, Lottie cried wildly. She refused to let Heidi leave, clinging tightly to her. It was impossible to comfort or quiet her. In desperation, after half an hour, Heidi telephoned the mother of Dorrie's friend. The mother came right over, bringing Dorrie. Lottie was finally quieted with Dorrie's help and put to bed.

The next day Lottie's father felt that Lottie had to be punished for this behavior, but he was in a quandary over what to do. He talked seriously with Lottie, asking her to explain her behavior. Lottie could give no reason that her father found acceptable. She said she was scared of Gladys in the night—Gladys was dressed in grey and looked like a shadow (Gladys was a young, colored college girl and Lottie's favorite sitter at the time)—she needed Dorrie and she needed Heidi. Mr Baker told her that he would have spanked her if he had been there but he could not spank her now for something she had done yesterday. He told her what the punishment would be: during the next two days, for any misbehavior on her part, instead of talking to her about it,

131

scolding her, as he usually did, he would "slap" her (a spank on the buttocks). Lottie was very serious but she did not cry. She asked for many explanations of *how long* this punishment would last. She could not understand what a duration of two days meant. He had to explain in terms of the sequence of meals and morning, afternoon, and night just how long it would be. Lottie did, in fact, receive four or five slaps from him in those two days, which she accepted solemnly without tears.

Mr and Mrs Baker believed that Lottie's comprehension of time (the future, duration, telling time) was behind for a child of her intellectual ability and fine number sense (she enjoyed simple addition and subtraction as well as counting almost to one hundred). When she was almost six she had memorized the days of the week. But if she were told what day today was, she could not say for sure what tomorrow would be. She was starting to learn how to tell the time, on the hour and at half-past. However, she was reluctant, showing much less interest in acquiring this skill than was usual for her in a learning situation.

Her greatest confusion about time involved Dorrie. On returning from school she always asked, "Is Dorrie home?" even though Dorrie came home for lunch half an hour after Lottie did *every* day. A few minutes after Dorrie left for school, when lunch was over, Lottie would ask, "Will Dorrie be coming now?" (Dorrie always returned from school three hours later.) Sometimes, in the early afternoon, Lottie would ask her mother: "Did we have lunch?"

One day, in the spring, Lottie told me that she had been sent out to the hall (in school) for talking and moving during resting:

I	How long did you stay out there?
LOTTIE	I don't know.
I	Was it just a few minutes or quite a while?
LOTTIE	I don't know. I stayed until music-time.

The major question of Lottie's five-year-old bedtime routine was to ask her mother: "When will Daddy, you, Heidi, Dorrie go to bed?" She used to be satisfied with the response: "Soon." But, shortly before her sixth birthday, she began to ask what time her parents would retire.

In general, Lottie's fifth year seems to have been relatively free of learning disturbances other than the one just described concerning the assessment of time—a disturbance that might have had its origins during the period of acute separation anxiety at the age of two.

LOTTIE AT EIGHT YEARS OF AGE

When Lottie was six and a half years old and in first grade, her family moved to another state; this necessitated changing schools in the middle of the year. The move involved an important development in Mr Baker's professional career which proved highly satisfying and positive with respect to both the conditions and the content of his work.

For many months Lottie and her sisters longed to return to their former home. They felt as if they were visitors rather than residents in the new community. Mrs Baker shared this reaction to some extent. During the first year and a half after the move, Lottie did not have special friends or playmates outside of school. She was, therefore, especially dependent for companionship on her sister Dorrie. Moreover, when Lottie became a second-grader at seven her mother returned to college as a part-time student; her plan was to complete her training so that by the time Lottie reached high school, Mrs Baker would be ready to work. She arranged to be away from home while Lottie was in school; nevertheless, the requirements of her studies reduced somewhat the time and energy available for the household and for Lottie.

One of the main hardships imposed by the move was the separation of the two families—the Bakers' and mine—that had lived in such close proximity for so many years. However, I

K

and various members of my family visited the Bakers three times during the two-year period (from January 1961) and Caron spent the summer of 1962 with the Baker family. It was during the third visit, in January 1963, that I observed Lottie at eight and a half years of age and obtained separate interviews with her mother and her father.

7 January 1963. Interview with the mother

(What is Lottie like, at eight and a half?) We've been waiting for the quiet period that is supposed to come between six and nine. It never has come—no "latency". Lottie has never been quiet since six months of age. She is always in conflict, always in turmoil, something seething within.

She's in bad with her father. He's very sensitive to her—I feel I have to mediate. He gets annoyed at her the way you would with an adult. (What does Lottie do?) She is provocative, argumentative, always correcting. She will not permit any errors. If you say one thing and she doesn't expect it, or doesn't agree, she jumps in, "No, that's wrong. You said such and such. . . ." She doesn't pull out of it nicely. She's reluctant to admit she was wrong. No bigness.

(What about her attachment to Dorrie?) While it's as strong as, if not stronger than, ever—she's attempting to pull away, but not with a positive approach, with an angry one. She's not giving up the ghost without a fight. She's very argumentative. She elicits anger and fighting back from Dorrie—who is also trying to disentangle herself from her relationship to Lottie. Dorrie complains bitterly that half or more of the trouble she gets into with me is because of Lottie. Lottie provokes her, Dorrie reacts, and I will jump on Dorrie. Lottie can intimidate Dorrie. She holds a threat over Dorrie—that she will tell on her. Lottie *will* tattle. Dorrie is disappointed in Lottie; after Dorrie shares something with her, Lottie doesn't keep a secret. They're not all that bad. They have moments of very good play and rapport.

Dorrie comes down to a very childish level. They will play quite wildly, then Dorrie gets into difficulty. I get annoyed with Dorrie (who is almost twelve) for not pulling Lottie up to her level. Instead, she is pulled down by Lottie.

Lottie is not tactful. She is frank beyond the word frank. This is not off the top of her head, there's some calculation involved. Here's an example: Lottie was anxious to have a friend sleep overnight with her, an older girl in fourth grade. Dinner went well and they had a good evening. Dorrie was out—sleeping over with a friend of hers. Perhaps this was part of Lottie's drive to have someone stay over. Lottie and her friend, Vera, were using Dorrie's bedroom and this was a great thrill. They seemed very happy and played well, with Lottie dominating the situation. They got into bed. When I came in to them, I thought I saw tears in Vera's eyes. I questioned her. "Lottie said that there are spiders in this bed." To have said this to her friend—I don't know how she could have done it. I turned on Lottie, "How can *you* of all people frighten someone with spiders?" I was shocked. Lottie said, "But I was only teasing and she knew I was only teasing." Maybe Lottie was ridding herself of her own anxieties, but I thought it very tactless and unkind.

Lottie has called me very little at night; she rather turns to Dorrie. But the few times she has called me, it has been to complain about spiders and other bugs in her bed. I say to Lottie that we will spray in the morning. They are not big spiders—just little, useful ones. (Were there ever really spiders in the bed?) Once, when I told the maid to spray, she *did* find a nest of spiders. Lottie carefully examines and looks every night; such a compulsion getting ready for bed. It's not just delaying tactics. She still asks every night, "Where are you going to be, Mommy?" I have to tell her. I say I don't know —in the kitchen or the living room. I'll be around.

I've talked to Mr Baker about Lottie. I have the feeling that if this child has an artistic talent, then this is the kind of personality you would see in a very talented person. Perhaps she has a germ of something great—or it could be bad. When my mother describes my sister as a child—so difficult, so hard to manage, so *talented* in so many ways—without meaning to, I identify Lottie with my family; she looks more like my side. It will have been worth it, if it turns out to be something great. But I'd rather have her be a regular, fine individual. (What does Mr Baker think about this idea?) He laughs when we talk about it.

(How does Lottie feel about her father?) It's hard to tell, because she provokes him so much, so deliberately. He corrects her. Then she'll do it again a little while later. It's not that she's not trying—but not hard enough. She's not thoughtful enough about the consequences. She's not outwardly a physically aggressive child, but she's diabolically aggressive for an eight-year-old. She uses a shrewdness. For instance, scaring people: she'll hide behind the door, then come out and say, "Boo!" I can't stand it. I say, "You really scare me. You *can't* do it to me." I'll be doing the dishes, all of a sudden I'll turn around and she'll be standing there behind me. On the other hand, comes Hallowe'en, she *will* not put a mask on. When it's acceptable, she won't. She commented on a little boy, younger than she, wearing a mask, "Look! He's wearing a mask!" Dorrie does the scaring as well. Dorrie liked practical jokes—I sat her down: "I don't really like them. They're aggressive, *not* funny." She's cut it out with me. Father is a tease, but not a practical joker.

(What do you enjoy about Lottie?) At her best there's no one like her. Same as with my sister. But those times are not so frequent. I enjoy watching her esthetically. I'm a little awed by her. She can mimic. Her understanding and her quickness are remarkable—which, incidentally, do not come out in school.

Lottie has been unfortunate in school. This is not just an excuse. Her teachers have not been good. Perhaps another child could have done better. She is ambivalent about school. Her best time in school is what is called "sharing": each child tells about something he or she has done. Last year, half her marks were average and half above grade level. She is very good at arithmetic. She reads well, although she's not outstanding, but her capacity to *understand* what she reads, or what is read to her, is phenomenal. I'm reading *The Wind in the Willows* to her. When I try to explain difficult words, she is impatient: "Yes, yes, go on—I *know*." If I check on it, she *does* have a very good idea of the meaning. Words are still a very picturesque thing for her. It's quite a different story in art work. With Heidi having a real artistic flair, and Dorrie—intellectually and with instruction—doing fine things, Lottie still makes the same Christmas tree card every year. She recently made a polka-dot design, copied from her pajamas, and presented it as a picture—expecting admiration for it. She does not express imagination in drawing at all.

(How is Lottie doing in school this year?) Lottie works at a little above grade level. But she says she gets "Cs"—translating the words into the letters used in upper-grade report cards. She is not dismayed. She's had real clashes with her teacher. Her teacher is a young, attractive woman. We spoke to her about Lottie at the parent-teachers meeting—she said, and it built up as she went along: "Things will be all right, but I have trouble with Lottie. If there's anything I can't stand it's a child who *clings* to me, at my apron strings, begging for attention—which *Lottie* does *not* need." The teacher said all this in a very disturbed manner—I was aghast. The teacher used the term "currying favor" in talking about Lottie. This teacher looks a bit like a beloved, young adult cousin who spent part of the summer with us. Lottie and she had a very intense, teasing relationship. Perhaps that explains in part why Lottie tried so hard to get this teacher's attention in this way. (What did you do about it?) We told Lottie not to try to get on her teacher's good side this way—not to pull on her to "see me, see me". Lottie got the point. She did change. In this case she realized. We did consider a switch.

But the school set-up is changing shortly and Lottie may get a different teacher.

With this little girl I have the feeling that she has to face up to these things—different kinds of people. To have her work it out herself enables her to achieve something. Her education may suffer. But I don't need her report card to tell me about her intellect. She has not had a teacher whom I have respected since the move. The second half of first grade here was very bad. The teacher shouted. I felt even then that it was better for Lottie to work it through with the teacher than to pull her out of the situation. The reward of coming out of the situation, of managing, was enough. I do it out of confidence in her abilities and strength.

(What about friends?) There are all kinds of children she's interested in, for various reasons—even just to have the chance to watch a lot of TV. "We watched TV the whole afternoon," she'll say, provokingly, when she comes home. At home TV is not such a driving force. They don't watch so much. Lottie will say, "There's nothing worth while", and not watch. She's still frightened of certain programs—which I find silly—but much less than before. She will say happily while watching, "I'm going to have nightmares over this." I'll suggest she leave then. But she won't stop watching. This is very much the way Dorrie is. Lottie's friends are almost all older than she. Partly this is accidental, there are no third-graders around.

(What about the piano?) More and more of Lottie's spare time is spent at the piano. My idea originally was that since Heidi plays piano and Dorrie the flute, Lottie should have another instrument. But she really pushed for piano. It's been only three months now. She's taken to it fantastically. It's rewarding to her and to me. She is very good at it. She'll practise any chance she gets—even without the piano, she'll play on her hands. Her teacher, a man, thinks she is very remarkable. A book that others take a year on, she gets through in three months. He gives her a lot of work: "When one has a talent, practising is a joy." Lottie looks forward to her lessons. She puts the appropriate chord, with a flourish, at the end of every scale. This she added herself. She has a good ear. Her father played a piece just once for her; she played a good part of it back, almost perfectly. There is no strain here. She is so matter-of-fact about it. I pick her up for her lesson right after chorus in school, we dash over to her teacher's house. She says, "Hi!", washes her hands and starts to play immediately. She whips through everything. Her teacher will say, "Did I give you all this? You had time?" She uses everyone for her music. A friend of her father's has the same teacher—as does Heidi—on the same day; he just started piano. They're in direct competition. They play for each other. She makes up compositions for her teacher and he encourages her. "By the way," she'll say casually, "I've written another piece." The teacher writes down her pieces for her. Such delight and pleasure she gets out of it. When she gets into difficulty, instantly she'll go to the piano. No limit, no chore, it's a real release. It must be extremely rewarding to her. And I feel very good about it too. I know very little about the piano. Lottie gets help from Heidi. They also argue about who gets the piano for practising. I allow myself the pleasure of staying at Lottie's lessons. But soon I plan not to stay.

(What about Lottie's reactions to separations?) She still has trouble saying 'Bermuda'—or rather, something comes out before the word. Bermuda has come up now and then in conversations between her father and me. Something—perhaps a flower—reminds us of our vacation there four years ago, when the girls stayed with you for five days. I told Lottie about the Bermuda vacation only recently and I've noticed that she stumbles around when she tries to say the word, or she avoids saying it altogether. It's funny that Heidi, who was nearly thirteen at the time, now remembers the Bermuda vacation as having lasted a very long time— two weeks or so!

(What about crying?) I think Lottie cries very little, less than you might expect. She cries only when she is really physically hurt or when her feelings are very hurt.

(Is apple juice still important to Lottie?) Exactly as it has always been. Part of her happiness at mealtime can come from a brand new can of apple juice, or from just having everyone drink it. At times I get terribly annoyed and I want to wean her from it, I don't know why. She has grown up to the point where she'll say, if we're out of it, "Will you get some?"—rather than make a big fuss. She is very particular about brands, only one or two will do. She can tell the difference. I once poured a bottle of different apple juice into a can of her kind. There was a startle effect—but she didn't say anything. Then I told her.

(How is Lottie's sense of time?) Very good. But when she talks about her estimate of how long things go on, she greatly exaggerates. She uses words like "millions, trillions, thousands". But she is also very accurate: "I got up at two o'clock. I saw the time. No one was around, and I went right back to sleep. Then I got up at ten after seven." This is part of the accuracy that she has—and demands of others. Dorrie would be more likely to exaggerate, to say she hadn't slept a wink all night.

The routine at night, getting ready for bed, she handles completely by herself. She wears more clothing at night than in the day—socks and clean pants under her warm pajamas. She washes, and then cleans up the bathroom sink. She makes sure that the water doesn't drip. She touches every drawer in her room to make sure it's closed; she makes sure that the closet door is shut. She checks the mattress. Sometimes she'll go through it all twice—especially if she has been interrupted. Sometimes, after I sing her the bedtime songs, she'll ask me to close the closet door. But it's already been done.

Lottie doesn't like boys at all. I correlate it with Dorrie's feelings. When Dorrie liked a boy some months ago, Lottie did too. When Dorrie changed, so did Lottie.

Last winter, when Lottie was seven and a half, she had her appendix out. She often says, "I wish I could have my appendix out again. It was so great!" Because of special circumstances, she was able to come home after only twelve hours at the hospital. About her scar—which is a beauty— she'll say, "How ugly it is. I can't bear to look at it. It's disgusting." I say, "It's a fine one." She admits she was scared— but it was great. They gave her a gift at the hospital, a hand puppet. She adored it. For a long time afterwards she took it to bed with her. There was a ghastly couple of days when she lost it; she tormented herself with losing it. It was finally found. Now it's not important to her any more.

(What about fears?) Lottie is afraid of bugs of all kinds. Dorrie is too. "Ugh," Dorrie will say, "it makes me feel crawly all over!" Both of them make a big fuss over insects. Lottie takes horseback riding lessons and I think she fears the horses, although she won't admit it. Some of it is justifiable—at almost every lesson, some child gets thrown. (Why did you decide to give Lottie horseback riding lessons?) Because Dorrie and Caron had had them all last summer and Lottie accepted this. She had held off pushing for them, even though she wanted to ride very much. It was a reward.

We have wonderful moments together, she and I. The reading moments. We read to each other. She's quiet and thoughtful. There are more and more good moments between us. But they come up at unexpected times. Her father has more trouble with the time he spends with her. I'm taken aback by things coming up suddenly—unexpectedly, with no warning, and therefore unavoidable. They come out of nowhere—just when things are going great guns. It's as if she said, "That's enough of that good stuff. Let's get things moving more."

She had a personality change when she stopped taking her nap. She was a quiet, docile, contained, contented, easy baby. Just before she was a year old, she stopped taking a nap. I continued to put her to bed, but she wouldn't go to sleep. Gradually she was not napping any more—winding herself up, tighter and tighter, and then she took off.

9 January 1963. Interview with the father

(How do you think of Lottie?) I think of her as a very attractive, physically attractive, child—petite, sweet-looking, tremendously animated (especially facial characteristics), with sparkle and a dynamic quality. And with these positive qualities come others—part and parcel of the positive. She is headstrong, self-willed, and sullen; she has very fast mood swings, and they're shallow. She doesn't even cry with depth of feeling. She may cry for effect as well as from feeling. If you gave all these things numbers, and weighed them on a scale, you would come out with a very frequently difficult-to-live-with child, despite good qualities.

In my experience, one of the things that happens with children of this type is that they go from one phase right into another. There are no breaks, no rest, no easing up of pressure on themselves or on the family. Often this is an easier age to get along with —I don't like the term "latency"—but you don't get it with this kind of a child. Next thing you know, she'll be entering puberty.

She's "with it" all the time. When she pays attention, she is completely focused on you. Even when she seems not to pay attention, she still hears fifty per cent at least.

(How do you get along with Lottie?) I use two techniques that were not deliberate, originally—they were evoked from my feelings. Now they are more deliberate. When it's humanly possible to be warm and tender, I am. The rest of the time, I am very strict—much stricter than with Heidi or Dorrie. If I'm not, then she rides roughshod over the entire family until one does set a limit or stop her.

(Do you feel, as Mrs Baker does, that Lottie became the

way she is at about a year?) In contrast to Dorrie, as a baby Lottie was much calmer, an easy baby—Dorrie was colicky. As Lottie became mobile and a thinking, verbal child—and this was very early—we realized this was an extremely active child. All of these things entered in; it was not a sudden change. Whereas Dorrie has become more calm, sober, and steady—in outward appearance. By the same token, perhaps Lottie has plateaued now at this high level, the slope has lowered a bit. I would draw the starting-point at eight to twelve months. Remember, this is a child who can sit for two hours in the morning with a group of dolls or a book. It is not consistent to try to make the claim that she is more "high-strung" than the average. This is *not* a high-strung, sensitive, delicately balanced child. She is hardy, resilient, tough—but high-spirited.

(How do you expect Lottie will develop?) We're looking forward with expectation to a fine human being out of this. (What about your wife's feeling that Lottie may be an unusually talented person?) Well, she has put twice as much into this child and so she feels something very unusual should come of it. (What do you enjoy about Lottie?) I enjoy her very much on occasion. Her way of seeing things is remarkable. She has a very different way of perceiving situations. She is always able to "ham it up", to dramatize. It's amusing. I'm just as capable of being extremely irritable with her— more than with the others. (What is her attitude to you?) Her attitude to me seems to be something like: You know, Daddy, I'd really like you if you weren't so strict.

It's more disturbing for her to be one of three—not just because of position, being the youngest, but because of the kind of person she is. It would have been easier for her to be one of two—or, better yet, one of one. It's hard for her to share— anything.

Each of the three girls has a particular role in the family: Heidi is outstanding for her goodness, Dorrie for her intellect —and what was left for Lottie? She has a made a unique place for herself based on the forceful and dramatic qualities of her personality.

(What about Lottie's relationship to Dorrie?) It's hard to analyze, especially because the two children are interacting. There was a period of relative stability in the relationship, when Lottie was five, six, and seven. But now there is a change coming on, a moving apart. When they are getting on well, it's very good. When it's bad, it's very bad—they have to be separated. Dorrie started vying with Lottie's friends, taking Lottie's friends away from her. But Lottie still looks up to Dorrie and admires her.

(How is Lottie's understanding of time?) It is close to normal. However, a wait for her of two minutes is as a wait of four minutes for another child.

January 1963. Observations of Lottie at eight and a half

Shortly after I arrived, Dorrie and Lottie told me that I was "the good mother" and Mrs Baker was "the bad mother". Mrs Baker, they said, always "yelled" at them and ordered them about—whereas I, they maintained, never did anything like that. When I demurred, they insisted on their distinction. "Mommy *never* lets me win!" Lottie exclaimed. They returned to this half-joking theme several times during my five-day visit. Although Dorrie and Lottie shared this attitude, they diverged on their specific complaints. Dorrie objected to being "saddled with Lottie", while Lottie deplored being told what to do all the time: "Mommy makes me wear a dress that I hate and she only lets me wear sneakers to school once a week."

I asked Lottie how she liked school. She shrugged her shoulders, "It's all right." Although she was apparently capable of superior performance, Lottie was doing work at a level only slightly above average. Outside of school, however, she was an eager pupil, enjoying the mastery of new skills and activities.

At her riding lesson, she proudly demonstrated her prowess to her mother and me. She sat well on her horse and trotted with ease, without any outward sign of apprehension. Spurred on, no doubt, by her sister's passion for horses (for months Dorrie had been haunting the nearby stables), Lottie had acquired considerable competence, despite the unspoken fear of riding her mother had discerned.

In her living room, Lottie showed me an intricate jumping game she had learned from a friend. A series of complicated steps, in prescribed order, was executed by the feet—catching and releasing a taut circle of knotted rubber bands. Lottie performed the sequence lightly and quickly, explaining each step and correcting every error.

The piano was used by Lottie as though it were a new language, creatively and dramatically. She discovered transposing by herself and played her pieces in several different keys. She was particularly pleased with the modern, mocking effect she achieved by transposing just the treble clef of a piece. She enjoyed both practising alone and performing for an audience. When reprimanded, she rushed to the piano for solace. During her lesson, Lottie was poised, confident, and efficient—giving precise information about her work, playing solos and duets with equal aplomb, and eagerly asking for the next assignment.

At play, with other children and by herself, the age-level of Lottie's behavior was extremely varied. Sometimes she was motherly, affectionate, and dominating—as she was with a three-year-old boy who came to visit. Lottie's play with Dorrie most often involved physical activity—running, jumping, dancing, and singing. It tended to become louder and more boisterous as it went on. The duration of an attempt to play a more advanced game together—juggling—was brief. While Dorrie practised tossing a single ball, carefully following the instructions, Lottie quickly shifted to using two balls. Dorrie was scornful of Lottie's inability to wait for the next step, "You're doing it all wrong. You're not ready for two balls." Lottie protested strongly that she was doing it right. Shortly thereafter, the joint activity ceased.

In Lottie's room, the old, worn doll Honeybunch—her face lined with fine cracks—was still to be seen. A set-up of small dolls was ready for play: the oldest girl-doll was in charge of a hospital room of younger dolls, all girls, who were being hospitalized for either operations or broken bones. Lottie frequently played by herself with her hospital, taking expert care of the patients; feeding, sleeping, dressing, and medical routines predominated.

One evening at bedtime I asked Lottie if she would show me her appendix scar. The small, thin, white line she termed horrible and ugly. She went on to tell me how wonderful the operation was and how she wished she could have it again. "What other operations can people have?" she asked. "Perhaps another appendix? How about a kidney?" she persisted. (In a song Lottie was fond of singing, there was a line about Uncle Sidney losing his kidney.) I inquired what was wonderful about the operation. Lottie spoke about the beautiful Christmas tree in the hospital and the present she had been given there. She jumped out of bed to find the hand puppet to show me. She pointed out the mark she had made on the cloth body "where he had his appendix out". That night Lottie took the puppet to bed with her.

Lottie's favorite toy animal was a stuffed, pink snake—six feet long. By day it lay coiled on her pillow. Each night she arduously shoved it under the tightly tucked covers so that it stretched the length of the bed, lying next to her while she slept.

One night, Heidi—who was baby-sitting for Dorrie and Lottie—telephoned Mr Baker at the restaurant where he was dining with us, to say that Lottie was so unmanageable that she (Heidi) was unable to put her to bed. It took a sharp order from her father on the telephone to get Lottie to settle down. The next day Lottie was punished, despite her complaint that Heidi had mishandled her. Mrs Baker commented that Lottie tended to misbehave when she was left in the care of Heidi and other sitters. She did not feel that Lottie was anxious when her parents went away, even for periods of several days. However, Lottie often "acted up".

The last evening of our visit, we went for a walk with the Baker family. Lottie interrupted a conversation between her mother and me to tell me a joke. I asked her to wait until we were finished. When she persisted, I said she would have to wait. Her reaction was very strong. She looked deeply hurt and disconsolate. She walked alone at a great distance behind us. She rebuffed my urging her to join us, saying she was looking at the moonlight. I told her that the conversation was finished and now she could tell me the joke. She retorted that it was an old one anyway, and she did not recount it. She finally came up to the group again, but not to rejoin Mrs Baker, Heidi, and myself. Rather, she rushed to take my husband's arm—continuing the walk with him, her father, and Dorrie. (I wondered whether she had seized on this incident because I was leaving the next morning; her reaction may have served both to anticipate the separation and to resolve the half-joking split between the "good" and the "bad" mother.) An hour later, at bedtime, Lottie was very affectionate once again.

PERSISTING TRENDS

The follow-up parent interviews and the observations of Lottie through the age of eight serve to confirm a basic assumption of the study, that this is a child whose behavior falls well within the normal range.

It may be worth while to note certain continuities from two to eight years of age—especially sequelae of new behaviors that arose out of the separation experience of entering nursery school (see Case Summary and Hypotheses in the preceding chapter). These continuities could be interpreted in a number of different ways. For example, they could be personality trends that would have become manifest during the third year of life irrespective of the separation experience. Or the continuities could be the outcome of behaviors that evolved specifically in solution to the nursery-school separation experience. There is also the possibility that an interaction is involved: incipient personality trends could have been reinforced by the events of the first year at nursery school.

Although one cannot hope to unravel these threads with the kind of data this study affords, certain of the continuities can be pointed out. The relative weight to be given to separation experiences of the type that occurs when a child begins nursery school can be worked out only by other studies.

What has been the fate, six years later, of those reactions that were apparently evoked most directly by the nursery-school separation experience? Lottie's major defense, as we have seen, was the identification with her sister Dorrie, three years her senior. The explicit identification persisted throughout the year at home, until Lottie turned three, months after it was no longer manifest at nursery school. In the four years that followed, the attachment to Dorrie dominated Lottie's world. It remained the source of her greatest satisfactions, although she no longer claimed to 'be' Dorrie. At eight years of age, Lottie is still tightly bound to her next older sister. The admiration and emulation continue unabated, as well as the preference to be with Dorrie above anyone else. To be sure, there are quarrels, tattling, and other negative features in the relationship which have now become more pronounced. Despite the increasingly overt ambivalence, Dorrie continues to be—second only to her mother—the main person in Lottie's life.

Lottie resorted to another defense in her initial efforts to cope with nursery-school separation: pseudo-elation. She substituted laughter for tears. With jokes, songs, and exaggerated gaiety, she denied her need to cry. Lottie's struggle with crying extended over two-thirds of the year. The sobbing outbursts for her mother, which came after she gave up her denial defenses, were followed by a period of renewed holding back of tears. Then, when Lottie resumed crying in school at her mother's departure, she spoke

148

about it continually—predicting and reporting it every day for many weeks. Gradually it became routine and dwindled to token tears. The first day that Lottie did not cry at all, she announced it as a great triumph.

At eight, Lottie is the humorist of the family—a skilled mimic and inveterate teller of jokes. It is often difficult to know whether or not to take her seriously. Characteristic of Lottie's behavior is a wry, tongue-in-cheek quality combined with a tendency to dramatize. As for crying, Lottie sheds tears partly for effect—her father says—and she usually does not cry with depth of feeling. Her mother remarks that Lottie cries less than would be expected.

Finally, some of Lottie's direct emotional reactions to separation from her mother can be traced from the age of two to eight. Throughout the period that the two-year-old Lottie was attempting to cope with nursery school, the longing for her mother during home separations was greatly intensified. At five, she passed through a new phase in which she constantly worried in advance about having to wait for her mother. Lottie had the obsessional fear, while waiting for her mother, that something bad might have happened to her. Later that same year came the unusual incident in which Lottie broke into such uncontrollable weeping when left alone with a baby-sitter that Dorrie had to be sent for to calm her down. Although at eight years of age there are no longer any overt signs of anxiety, Lottie frequently misbehaves, becoming very difficult to manage, when her parents leave her with a sitter. Most often it is Heidi who is in charge— the older sister against whose authority Lottie has intermittently protested since the age of two.

Thus the dominant emotional reactions and defenses that the two-year-old child resorted to in response to the nursery-school separation experience seem to have their counterparts six years later, when she was last observed. Could it be that a mild, carefully handled separation from the mother at the age of two is capable of having lasting effects on the ways in which a child's personality develops?

APPENDIX A

List of Nursery-School Sessions

	Autumn 1956		Winter 1957		Spring 1957
1.	20 September	23.	8 January	39.	9 April
2.	27 September	24.	15 January	40.	11 April
3.	2 October	25.	22 January	41.	18 April
4.	4 October	26.	24 January	42.	23 April
5.	9 October	27.	31 January	43.	25 April
6.	11 October	28.	5 February	44.	30 April
7.	16 October	29.	7 February	45.	2 May
8.	18 October	30.	14 February	46.	7 May
9.	23 October	31.	19 February	47.	9 May
10.	30 October	32.	21 February	48.	14 May
11.	1 November	33.	26 February	49.	16 May
12.	6 November	34.	28 February	50.	21 May
13.	8 November	35.	5 March	51.	23 May
14.	13 November	36.	7 March		
15.	15 November	37.	12 March		
16.	27 November	38.	14 March		
17.	29 November				
18.	4 December				
19.	6 December				
20.	11 December				
21.	13 December				
22.	18 December				

APPENDIX B

An Observation of Lottie Five Months
before starting Nursery School

Even before the age of two, Lottie exhibited the intensity and persistence that are so characteristic of her behavior. Never placid, or content with things as they are, she is one who 'reaches for the moon'. The following record was obtained five months before the start of nursery school.

21 May 1956. Record of Lottie's discovery of the moon at twenty-two months

Lottie and her sisters spent the night at my house while her parents were away. We all went out for dinner to a restaurant.

On coming out of the restaurant, I pointed out the moon to Lottie. She was immediately enthralled. She kept looking at it and making remarks: "Lottie see it. Take it down! Lottie hold it!" I explained that it was far, far away and could not be taken down. Lottie kept looking at the moon and talking about it. I had to carry her to the car and promise that she would see it again as soon as we reached home.

During the short ride Heidi said that she could see the moon from the car. Lottie tried but she couldn't. She was very excited and had to be told several times that she would see it soon.

When the girls got out of the car at my house, they all rolled in the grass, as they often do. I picked Lottie up and, on the way into the house, pointed out the moon to her. It was hard to see it between the branches of a tree. But when Lottie finally glimpsed it, she did not want to go in: "Moon! Lottie have it! Take it down!" I carried her in, telling her about the birthday cake the girls were going to serve (in honor of Queen Elizabeth).

I removed her snowsuit, Lottie objecting. Kaye went outside again and Lottie cried: "Want to see the moon! Want to see Kaye!" I took her into the bedroom where she could see the moon out of the window from the bed. Lottie was very excited, talking and reaching for the moon.

Despite my urgings to come in for some cake, Lottie stayed alone on the bed. I went back to get her a few minutes later for the cake ceremony. She was still moon-gazing. I took her into the kitchen, but she refused to eat any cake in order to get back to the moon.

She wanted me to come back with her. It was now fairly dark in the room. While I undressed her Lottie talked continuously about the moon: "Take it down. Lottie hold it. Lottie hold it on her lap!" I explained again about its size and distance. Lottie: "Lottie too little. Apple juice take moon?" I laughed: "Not apple juice." Lottie: "Apple juice hold it? No. Apple juice in frigerator."

When she was ready for bed Lottie objected to having the blind drawn: "Want to see moon!" But finally she was carried to her bed and accepted going to sleep.

REFERENCES

AINSWORTH, M. D. & BOWLBY, J. (1954). 'Research Strategy in the Study of Mother-Child Separation.' *Courrier*, **IV**, 3.

BOWLBY, J. (1951). *Maternal Care and Mental Health*. Geneva: World Health Organization Mon. No. 2. U.K.: H.M.S.O.; U.S.A.: Columbia Univ. Press.

BOWLBY, J., ROBERTSON, J. & ROSENBLUTH, D. (1952). 'A Two-Year-Old Goes to Hospital.' *Psychonal. Study Child*, **VII**.

BURLINGHAM, D. & FREUD, A. (1942). *Young Children in War-Time*. London: Allen & Unwin.

BURLINGHAM, D. & FREUD, A. (1944). *Infants without Families*. London: Allen & Unwin.

FREUD, A. (1942). *The Ego and the Mechanisms of Defence*. London: Hogarth.

FREUD, A. (1949). 'Nursery School Education—Its Uses and Dangers.' *Child Study Quart.*, Spring.

GOLDFARB, W. (1943). 'Effects of Early Institutional Care on Adolescent Personality.' *J. exper. Educ.*, **12**.

HEINICKE, C. M. (1956). 'Some Effects of separating Two-Year-Old Children from their Parents: A Comparative Study.' *Human Relations*, **9**, 2.

KUHMERKER, L. R. (1954). 'Acclimatization to Initial School Experiences.' Yale University Ph.D. Thesis.

ROBERTSON, JAMES. (1953). Film: *A Two-Year-Old goes to Hospital*. London: Tavistock Clinic; New York: New York University Library.

ROBERTSON, JAMES. (1958). *Young Children in Hospital*. London: Tavistock Publications; New York: Basic Books.

ROBERTSON, JOYCE. (1956). 'A Mother's Observations on the Tonsillectomy of her Four-Year-Old Daughter. With Comments by Anna Freud.' *Psychoanal. Study Child*, **XI**.

WOLF, K. M. (1945). 'Evacuation of Children in Wartime: A Survey of the Literature, with Bibliography.' *Psychoanal. Study Child*, **I**.

WOLFENSTEIN, M. (1954). *Children's Humor: A Psychological Analysis*. Glencoe, Illinois: The Free Press.

INDEX

ambivalence, 25, 36, 66, 90, 119, 148
anal interest, 50, 69, 74f, 76, 93
anger, 37, 46, 90, 102f, 109
animals, aggression toward or fear of, 22, 23, 25, 27, 46f, 49, 63, 72, 87f, 91, 94f, 96, 98f, 103, 105, 108, 125, 135, 141
anxiety, *see* fears; separation
appendectomy, 141, 146
authority, resistance to, 41f, 43, 83, 90, 100, 149

bedtime ritual, 40f, 65, 66, 69, 85, 91, 98, 133, 135, 140, 146
birthday party, 77, 86, 93, 101
biting, 91, 103
    fear of, 87, 91, 95, 119
    see also animals
body damage, fantasies of, 49f, 76, 118
Bowlby, John, 4
boys, attitude to, 20, 25, 63, 72, 105, 108, 126, 140f, 145

children, relationship with, *see* peer relationships
clinging, 20, 23, 38, 57, 81, 87, 95, 102, 116, 131
clothing, *see* dressing and clothing
compulsiveness, 64f, 69, 135, 140
confess, need to, 73
crying, 20, 54, 57f, 71, 78, 79, 86, 87f, 95, 97, 105, 116, 117f, 148f

death, 95, 96, 120, 125, 128f
defenses, 25, 34, 36f, 38, 40f, 46f. 48, 49, 54ff, 59, 70, 79f, 115f, 117, 118f, 148f
    see also denial; elation, pseudo-; identification
denial, as defense, 38, 43, 54, 55, 71, 80, 114ff, 122

dependency, *see* clinging; mother; separation
destructive behavior, 37, 40, 58, 90, 97f
displacement, 90f
dolls, 21, 30, 39, 48, 72, 88, 126, 130, 146
    as surrogates, 36, 38, 48
drawing, *see* painting and drawing
    of a person, 100
dressing and clothing, 35, 37, 42, 51, 60, 61, 63, 65, 69, 73, 80, 82, 83, 84f, 90, 92, 95, 99, 100, 103, 108, 118, 140, 144

elation, pseudo-, 43, 54ff, 115, 116, 148f
empathy, with other children, 44f

family, Lottie's position in, 27, 143f
fantasy, 25, 50, 76, 88, 100, 105, 109f, 119, 128, 130, 146
father, Lottie's, 18, 26, 28, 65f, 70, 79, 83, 92, 93, 97, 118, 126, 129, 130, 131f, 134, 136
    at school, 35, 80f, 87, 89, 98, 99, 105
    view of Lottie, 142ff
fathers, other, 62f, 64, 66, 73, 100, 126, 147
fears, 49f, 87, 91, 94f, 98f, 105, 119, 125, 128, 141
feeding, early, 32
    see also food and drink
food and drink,
    at home, 11ff, 19, 32, 53f, 77f, 84, 92, 99
    at school, 24, 52f, 62, 67, 104, 105f
    juice, 54, 62, 95, 130f, 140
future, concept of, 101, 120f

God, 130
gratification, delayed, 99, 101, 120
grudge, holding a, 65, 104, 147

154